*Critical Guides to French Texts*

84 Saint-Exupéry: Vol de nuit *and* Terre des hommes

*Critical Guides to French Texts*

EDITED BY ROGER LITTLE, WOLFGANG VAN EMDEN,
DAVID WILLIAMS

SAINT-EXUPÉRY

# Vol de nuit *and*
# Terre des hommes

**S. Beynon John**

Formerly Reader in French
University of Sussex

© Grant & Cutler Ltd
1990
ISBN 0-7293-0318-7

I.S.B.N. 84-599-2928-0

DEPÓSITO LEGAL: V. 251 - 1990

Printed in Spain by
Artes Gráficas Soler, S. A., Valencia

for

GRANT & CUTLER LTD
55-57, GREAT MARLBOROUGH STREET, LONDON W1V 2AY

# Contents

# Prefatory Note

BECAUSE a number of school and college editions of both these texts exist, some of which are out of print or difficult to obtain, I have chosen an edition which is cheap and widely available in current paperback reprints:

*Vol de nuit* ('Collection Folio', Paris, Gallimard, 1988).

*Terre des hommes* ('Collection Folio', Paris, Gallimard, 1988).

Quotations from both these texts will normally be indicated by page reference alone but occasionally, for the sake of clarity, I refer to *VN* or *TH* followed by the relevant page number. Numerical references to Saint-Exupéry's *Carnets* are to specific entries in the notebooks and not to pages of the printed edition.

I am again grateful to the Advisory Editor, Professor Roger Little, for his patience, encouragement and vigilance, and to Nancy Fortescue of the University of Sussex Library for her unfailing efficiency and helpfulness, on this occasion as in the past.

# Introduction

P A R T of the continuing fascination which Antoine de Saint-Exupéry has for readers of the 1990s lies in the fact that he revives for us in graphic terms what used to be called the 'romance of flight'. In our era of rocket-propelled journeys to the moon and wide-bodied jets ferrying passengers across continents with the regularity of buses, Saint-Exupéry's vivid accounts of flying by the seat of one's pants in the pioneering days of commercial aviation recover for us a vanished past and what was then a thrilling new dimension of human experience.

Yet it is fair to say that if Saint-Exupéry had been nothing but a professional flier putting his exploits on record, he would never have acquired the almost legendary reputation already granted to him by the French public in the 1930s, a legend reinforced by the mysterious manner of his death on 31 July 1944 when his plane disappeared off Corsica while on a reconnaissance mission during World War II. Though his zest for flying, his technical knowledge, personal courage and powers of endurance were never in question, Saint-Exupéry was a notoriously erratic pilot, both absent-minded and prone to accidents. As a test pilot for the firm of Latécoère near Toulouse (1932-33), he was careless about detail and faulty in his judgement. On one occasion, he took off without properly closing the cockpit door so that it was wrenched off in flight and fell to earth. On another (21 December 1933), he was nearly drowned when he ditched a seaplane in the bay of Saint-Raphaël. At the end of December 1935, in the course of his hastily prepared attempt on the Paris-Saigon air record, Saint-Exupéry and his mechanic made a crash-landing at night in the Libyan desert and were only rescued in the nick of time by travelling Bedouin. Later still, in February 1938, in his attempt to fly from Newark (New Jersey) to Tierra del Fuego, Saint-Exupéry's overladen plane crashed on take-off at Guatemala and he was left in a semi-coma with serious injuries.

These mischances and misjudgements simply illustrate the physical and psychological strains and the risks to life and limb to which Saint-Exupéry was exposed in his own experiences of flying, and which were inseparable from the peculiarly intimate union of pilot and plane that characterised the relatively small and fragile aircraft of the pioneering days of commercial aviation. Secondly, they point to a career as a flier which, in its range of skills and achievements, cannot really compare with the great pioneers of the 1920s and 1930s: Saint-Exupéry's own comrades, Jean Mermoz and Henri Guillaumet; or Charles Lindbergh, Amy Mollison and Jean Batty, among non-French fliers. In a word, and for all the qualities he brought to flying, Saint-Exupéry survives in the public mind and continues to be a magnetic figure for successive generations, not primarily because he was an outstanding airman but because he was a gifted writer. It is through his power to transform the raw material of flying into imaginative literature and to seize on its epic and exemplary qualities that we remember him and continue to be attentive to him.

In making something highly individual out of his own encounters in the air, Saint-Exupéry reclaimed an important area of human experience from the domain to which it had largely been confined until then: the recollections of fighter aces of the Great War. What makes *Vol de nuit* (1931) and *Terre des hommes* (1939) distinctive and memorable is the unique fashion in which they fuse together an extraordinarily vivid evocation of man's struggle with the elements and a vein of grave and persistent reflection on the moral and spiritual significance of human action in the world. As a result, each of these narratives embodies both a physical and moral landscape, the former appealing to the period taste for travel books. In exploring Saint-Exupéry's imaginary world in *Vol de nuit* and *Terre des hommes,* I shall want to look, in particular, at the relationship between fiction and autobiography, at the themes and values which dominate these narratives, and at the way in which language and imagery express the author's distinctive vision.

# 1

# Autobiography and Fiction

A s we have increasingly come to understand, autobiography
is itself a kind of fiction. The selection and ordering of
the events and experiences of an individual life, the language
in which they are framed, all subdue the random flow of life
to pattern and form and seek to impose significance on it. A
novel scarcely operates differently. So, though *Vol de nuit*
and *Terre des hommes* certainly draw heavily on Saint-
Exupéry's own lived experience, these autobiographical elements are not fundamentally different in kind from the more
obviously fictive elements. The borderline between autobiography and fiction is never wholly distinct.

In saying this, I am anxious not to minimise the kernel of
lived, personal experience which lies at the heart of both
books, but simply to indicate how autobiographical recollection already places the writer at a certain remove from brute
experience and so, easily shades off into the still more
distanced rendering of experience that we meet in the more
explicitly invented episodes – like the scene between the waking pilot and his wife in chapter X of *Vol de nuit* or the
revelations about inspector Robineau's private life that occur
in chapter VI. We may restate this in slightly different terms
and say that it will be appropriate to view *Vol de nuit,* and
even parts of *Terre des hommes,* as thinly fictionalised
autobiographical experience, so long as we recall that memory too is an artist and is involved in re-creating that past
to which we confidently appeal, as though it were a piece of
objective history quite outside ourselves. However, to show
the relationship between autobiography and fiction in these
two narratives, it will be convenient to identify the separate
strands while remembering that they are more completely

integrated in *Vol de nuit* than in *Terre des hommes,* where the fictional elements are greatly reduced.


( i )

*Vol de nuit* is a novel about the vicissitudes of night-flying as they affect a handful of pilots engaged in opening up South America to a regular mail-carrying service in the nineteen twenties and thirties. Saint-Exupéry's autobiographical experience enters *Vol de nuit* at two levels. First, it occurs by transposing the recollection of a real-life incident or series of incidents into a narrative that centres on the fatal last flight of an imagined pilot. Secondly, it operates at the level of the writer's hidden desires and inner contradictions in such a way as to shape significant aspects of the narrative. The lines between these two levels of experience are persistently shifting and blurred in the novel.

It will be helpful to begin with the fate of Fabien. Saint-Exupéry's chief biographer, Curtis Cate, accepts that Fabien is based on the real-life pilot Elysée Négrin who was forced to ditch his plane in the La Plata river in May 1930 (*1,* p. 230). So Fabien is drawn in part from a single 'historical' individual whom Saint-Exupéry had got to know in Buenos Aires in the course of his duties as Director of Operations for the airline, Aeroposta Argentina, between 1929 and 1931. Of course, this does not exclude the possibility that, insofar as Fabien is characterised at all, something of Saint-Exupéry's observations of other fliers enters into his account of Fabien, just as details of other flights, including Saint-Exupéry's own, may form part of the one depicted in Fabien's last flight. Again, as some critics have suggested, Fabien's name, like Pellerin's or even Rivière's, may simply be emblematic of a way of life rather than a means of individuating particular airmen. In this sense, 'Fabien' may echo *faber* (as in the Latin *homo faber*) with its implication of 'maker' or 'craftsman'. Similarly, 'Pellerin' may be a near homonym for the French 'pèlerin' (pilgrim), just as 'Rivière' may echo 'la rive' (river bank) and carry a suggestion of a mooring-place and, by extension, a safe landing. Such acts of symbolic naming undermine the notion that we are dealing with specific individuals, even if some part of them and their troubles is culled from actual experience. Indeed, it might be said that, in this process of naming, Saint-Exupéry is already moving beyond the 'historical' person on whom he is drawing. Fabien does, of course, die, but his fate may owe less to Saint-Exupéry's desire to record the death of one particular flier than to his desire to symbolise the risks and dangers that attach to the careers of all mail pilots in this pioneering period. In such a death, it could be said, Saint-Exupéry is enabled to memorialise and pay homage to those fliers who actually lost their lives, and to dignify and elevate the profession he himself had elected to follow.

This last seems to me to have been an especially strong impulse in Saint-Exupéry's life, and it is not difficult to understand why. He himself came, on his father's side, from an ancient aristocratic family with its origins in Toulouse – a country squire, Raymond de Saint-Exupéry, is mentioned in monastic records as early as 1235 (*1,* p. 20). But, in more recent times, the family had gone down in the world and Comte Jean de Saint-Exupéry, Antoine's father, who died in March 1904 when the child was not yet four, was an employee of an insurance company. Antoine himself, who received a conventional education in a series of Catholic boarding schools designed to prepare the children of the gentry for entry into the army and navy, failed to pass the entrance examination for the college for naval cadets at Brest (*1,* p. 46), and after a period of compulsory military service (1921-22), drifted into a series of uncongenial and unsuccessful jobs, notably as a production supervisor at the Boiron tile factory and as a salesman for Saurer lorries at their Suresne works on the outskirts of Paris (*1,* p. 90). These failures, coupled with the traumatic breaking off of their engagement by Louise de Vilmorin, beautiful daughter of a rich, aristocratic Parisian family, seem to me to supply the key to Saint-Exupéry's later impassioned conception of commercial aviation as a sort of new chivalry of the air. In the activity of flying, this impoverished young aristocrat, temperamentally at loggerheads with what he saw as the institutionalised mediocrity and corruption of the French Third Republic, found a way of rising, literally and symbolically, above the world which appeared to have no proper place for him. His early failures and the sense they gave him of being relegated to the margins of society, supply the powerful psychological impulses which inform his career as an airman and determine the exalted tone and sense of moral aspiration which mark all that he writes about the work of the airline. In fact, it is not too much to say that both *Vol de nuit* and *Terre des hommes* reflect Saint-Exupéry's persistent tendency to project aristocratic values and attitudes, frustrated in his early personal experience of French society, on to the activity of flying commercial aircraft. That is an aspect of the novels I shall examine in detail later.

Confirmation of the degree to which *Vol de nuit* embodies direct, autobiographical experience, even if inflected and transposed, can be found at several points in the novel. Most striking, in the sense of most vivid and transparent, is the way in which Pellerin's encounter with the cyclone as he undertakes the Chile run (chapters III and IV) and Fabien's battle with the hurricane as he flies up from Patagonia (chapters XII, XV, XVI), both draw on Saint-Exupéry's own flight in April 1930 from Trelew to Comodoro Rivadavia, a Patagonian town roughly half-way between Buenos Aires and Tierra del Fuego. It was on this flight that he was buffetted by the 150 mph winds of a cyclone (*1*, p. 179). If I refer to these fictional episodes as 'transparent', it is because we have got Saint-Exupéry's own account of his experiences and can see for ourselves the affinities between the episodes depicted in *Vol de nuit* and the incidents and language of the later autobiographical text. This text was originally inserted as an additional chapter ('The Elements') in *Wind, Sand and Stars,* the English translation of *Terre des hommes,* before appearing in French as 'Le pilote et les puissances naturelles' in the newspaper *Marianne* (16 August 1939).[1] Here I think it

---

[1] I use the text reprinted in *Cahiers Saint-Exupéry,* I (Paris, Gallimard, 1980), 29-40.

might be illuminating not simply to indicate how the account of Saint-Exupéry's real-life experience is echoed in the fictional rendering of the storms endured by Pellerin and Fabien, but also to note how the language and imagery of his recollections already fictionalise the lived experience by simultaneously ordering, distancing and intensifying it.

Saint-Exupéry's recollections, written, it must be remembered, years after the events they describe, open on an almost confessional note: 'Le cyclone dont je vais parler est bien l'expérience la plus saisissante dans sa brutalité qu'il m'ait été donné de subir...' (p. 29). This leads one to expect a piece of plain unvarnished testimony, but this reaction is almost instantly corrected when the writer turns to a literary model in order to explain the difficulties of communicating the immediacy of any overwhelming physical experience. He notes that in Conrad's description of a typhoon, the great novelist actually baulks before the task of describing the agitation of the elements and concentrates on the effects produced by the typhoon on the Chinese emigrants below decks (p. 29). In fact, this is a travesty of Conrad's marvellously graphic account of a hurricane in chapters 3-5 of *Typhoon*, but I am only interested here in the use to which Saint-Exupéry puts his faulty recollection of that novel. He admits to understanding the feeling of impotence felt by a writer when confronted with the task of finding a language adequate to conveying the fury of the elements without falling into a kind of verbal excess: 'passé une certaine mesure, je ne sais plus décrire la violence des remous qu'en multipliant des superlatifs qui ne charrient plus rien, sinon un goût gênant d'exagération. J'ai compris lentement la raison profonde de cette impuissance: on veut décrire un drame qui n'a pas existé. Si l'on échoue dans l'évocation de l'horreur, c'est que, l'horreur, on l'a inventée après coup, en revivant les souvenirs. L'horreur ne se montre pas dans le réel' (p. 30).

In a word, brute experience does not itself constitute a 'drame communicable'. At the height of a given extremity of experience, man is too involved in physical action to be aware of its emotional or dramatic significance. It is only by narrating this action subsequently that it can be seen as dramatic or moving: 'Mais le drame physique lui-même ne nous touche que si l'on nous montre son sens spirituel' (p. 40). This insight is not novel but it is clearly one to which Saint-Exupéry attaches importance. As readers, we too must accept that it establishes an aesthetic principle which is valuable for our understanding of his practice as a writer. Certainly it clinches the point I have tried to make that the distinction between autobiography and fiction is a tenuous one in Saint-Exupéry's work, if only because personal recollection itself represents a quasi-fictional reordering of the past and, if it is to be true to the original experience, will necessarily call on a fully expressive language – something different from artless rough notes or banal discursive prose.

If we now turn to a comparison between 'Le pilote et les puissances naturelles' and the description of the storms in *Vol de nuit,* this aesthetic principle is thrown into high relief. In 'Le pilote et les puissances naturelles' Saint-Exupéry emphasises the enormous physical strain of managing the aircraft's controls and illustrates this in the moment at which he tries to climb to safety. His hands do not respond to the messages from his brain though he clenches them hard and attempts, through a kind of incantation, to master himself: '"Je serre les mains..." Je me suis condensé tout entier dans cette phrase-là' (p. 37). This echoes Pellerin's tensing of his muscles as though in preparation for some impending ordeal (*VN,* p. 36) and in Fabien's even more vividly registered impression of finding his hands paralysed and oddly disconnected from the rest of his body, like flaccid bladders: 'Quelque chose d'étranger terminait ses bras. Des baudruches insensibles et molles' (*VN,* p. 138). Here, it might be said, an almost identical experience is given particularly intense and imaged expression in the case of Fabien whilst the imaginative representation of a similar experience suffered by Pellerin is less strong than that conjured up by Saint-Exupéry's autobiographical text. Elsewhere it is even more difficult to argue that Saint-Exupéry's own record is somehow more neutral or factual than the fictional versions of near-identical experiences.

For example, in 'Le pilote et les puissances naturelles', Saint-Exupéry, in attempting to suggest the deceptive calm that precedes the storm, refers to the preternatural blue of the sky in a vivid and effective image: 'cette lueur de couteau aiguisé' (p. 31). This way of associating the conventionally benign blue of the sky with the lethal possibilities of a sharp knife is no less 'literary' than Pellerin's perception of the apparent calm of the high Andes as resembling 'les châteaux morts' (*VN*, p. 35) under their mantle of snow. Indeed, in seeking to convey the sinister portents of the fearsome storm that is to come, Saint-Exupéry's recollection of 'une sorte de traînée de cendres' (p. 31) covering the mountain peaks is more concrete and effective than the fictional equivalent where Pellerin is content to note 'une poussière' infiltrating the air, though, admittedly, he later expands this.

When it comes to conveying the experience of a pilot caught up in the unleashed fury of the elements, Saint-Exupéry's own account registers powerfully the sudden shudder of the plane, motionless even though its engine is at full throttle, and the subsequent ordeal of being tossed helplessly up and down in such a way that it is no longer possible for the pilot to distinguish between vertical and horizontal: 'Je suis comme enfermé dans les coulisses d'un théâtre encombré de plans de décor' (p. 33). This strikingly novel image in which the confusion and bewilderment of the flier is likened to the shock of surprise experienced by someone faced with a jumble of false stage sets, is followed by another, equally suggestive of the world of illusion. As the earth gyrates wildly about him ('cette valse du paysage') the pilot strives to bring order out of chaos: 'je m'épuise à remettre sur pied un gigantesque château de cartes qui s'écroule indéfiniment' (p. 34). No images could better illustrate how, even in a fragment of direct autobiography, a process of literary distancing has taken place as the subject of these events steps back from their terrifying immediacy so as to convey to the reader the 'real' nature of his ordeal. As compared to this, Pellerin's references to the way in which the mountains 'seethe' ('semblait fermenter') around him and spew out snow like volcanoes (*VN*, pp. 36-37) are altogether more literal. As

for Fabien, his description of the hurricane and of losing any
sense of vertical or horizontal also depends less on the
suggestive obliquity employed in the autobiographical text
than on a kind of strong realism. Hence the directness of 'les
remous le soulevaient, dans ses cinq tonnes de métal, et le
basculaient' (*VN,* p. 135) is heightened, though still in a
naturalistic way, by what follows: 'toutes les masses du sol...
étaient comme arrachées de leur support, déboulonnées, et
commençaient à tourner, ivres, autour de lui' (*VN,* p. 137).
    Only in the final phase of this heroic duel between man
and the elements does one feel that Saint-Exupéry's narrative
comes nearer to a plain statement of testimony, as when he is
borne up by a violent gust of wind ('une sorte d'épanouisse-
ment'), only to be sucked down in a terrifying down-draught
that sends him plunging toward the sea before he is able
painfully to climb to 300 metres and to make for a calm
patch which he catches sight of some distance away. But at
the end of this passage, he too departs from the literal when
he describes the giant footprints which the cyclone has left on
the waves: 'là où les trombes descendantes se divisaient contre
les eaux en explosions horizontales' (p. 36). In *Vol de nuit*
Pellerin's account is equally plain as he describes how he is
suddenly hoisted up by powerful air-currents to a height of
7000 metres before being forced down to a level of 3000
metres and narrowly escaping collision with the mountains.
A degree of imaginative development colours this narrative
only when he recalls how the head of the cyclone is lost in
clouds of snow while its base sweeps over the plain like
volcanic lava: 'ainsi qu'une lave noire' (*VN,* p. 43). The most
haunting account of the final stage of this trial by the
elements is undoubtedly Fabien's, and it is so precisely
because it is an *imagined* death, handled in such a fashion as
to suggest a last farewell to those who are sacrificed to the
mission of carrying the mail. Of course, we do not see
Fabien's actual death but, as he climbs out of the heart of the
storm into a region bathed in blinding light, we share with
him this final, eerie and deceptive tranquillity: 'une part
de ciel inconnue et cachée comme la baie des îles bienheureu-
ses' (*VN,* p. 144). In rendering this glittering illusion of safety,

the fiction of *Vol de nuit* has expanded the sober facts of night flying by the pioneers of the Aeroposta Argentina so as to create a kind of radiant elegy. The imaginative force of this is of a different order from that of the descriptions contained in Saint-Exupéry's fragment of autobiography or the fictional representation of Pellerin's ordeal, but this difference does not derive primarily from the difference between testimony and fiction. Both forms *re-create* the original experience and both call on imaginative resources and a rich range of language.

Another illustration of how Saint-Exupéry's direct autobiographical experience infiltrates the text of *Vol de nuit* can be seen in his fictional characters. As has already been suggested, something of the real-life Elysée Négrin may lurk like a ghost behind Fabien. It is also plausible that something of Pellerin's undemonstrative professionalism and modesty may have been borrowed from the real-life Guillaumet (*5*, p. 50), that fine aviator who was Saint-Exupéry's close friend and colleague in the Latécoère airline. However, the crucial borrowing from life in *Vol de nuit* is to be found in the person of Rivière himself. It would not be right to say that he is nothing but a slavish copy from life but, undoubtedly, much of Didier Daurat, brilliant flying ace of the Great War and General Manager of the Latécoère Airline Company in Toulouse, enters into Saint-Exupéry's portrait of Rivière. There is ample testimony from those who worked under his command that Daurat was indeed an idealist, an ascetic and a severe disciplinarian who demanded heroic commitment, stringent self-discipline and self-sacrifice from his men, believing that such a regimen would give them a transcendent purpose in life and release what was finest in them. He combined this exacting gospel with great personal integrity and a genuine paternalistic concern for his men.

The fictional Rivière is given all these qualities and is also credited with being the first to conceive of the idea of night flights though, historically, this honour seems to belong to the record-breaking aviator, Mermoz (*3*, p. 157). Interestingly, however, when *Vol de nuit* first appeared in 1931 Saint-Exupéry was severely criticised by several of his old

colleagues in the airline for portraying Daurat (in the person
of Rivière) as an unfeeling and inflexible martinet (5, p. 124).
In this, they were unwittingly paying tribute to the triumph
of art over life, since they clearly feared that Rivière would,
in some way, be taken as more 'real' than Daurat. As we shall
also see, in chapter 3, such critics ignore the degree to which
the novelist uses Rivière as a focus for crystallising certain
notions of leadership, discipline and duty which intensely
interest him. In any event, criticism of the unfairness of
Saint-Exupéry's portrayal of Daurat (as Rivière) is misplaced
once the reader is truly attentive to the tone and emphases of
the text. Whatever criticisms readers may have about the
objective value of Rivière's ethos, the narrator of *Vol de nuit*
is clearly enthralled by him and in awe of his dominant
qualities.

Rivière emerges as a charismatic figure and it is tempting
to argue that, in the narrator's attitude to him, and especially
to the authority and hard discipline he imposes, we see the
symbolic expression of some of Saint-Exupéry's own deepest
needs. Here, in the figure of Rivière, is the father he never
had, one who inspires, guides but also chastises. Here, too, in
Rivière's code of discipline and obedience, is a sort of refuge
from the insecurity and weakened sense of self-esteem produced in Saint-Exupéry by his earlier failures. What is more,
in transferring Daurat/Rivière from Toulouse to Buenos
Aires, Saint-Exupéry, who was the actual Director of Operations for Aeroposta Argentina in the Argentinian capital,
symbolically reveals his aspiration to be another Daurat, to
be invested with that charisma, and to restore a kind of
aristocratic leadership to the world.

Another important facet of *Vol de nuit* is the way in
which it is obliquely related to Saint-Exupéry's childhood. In
a revealing letter to his mother, written from Buenos Aires in
January 1930,[2] the author recalls the comfort and protection
of the stove in his bedroom when he was a child and the

---

[2] Reprinted in *Lettres de Saint-Exupéry* (Paris, Le Club du Meilleur
Livre, 1960), 142.

delight he felt, when unwell, in occupying the large second bed in his mother's room:

> Je ne suis pas bien sûr d'avoir vécu depuis l'enfance. Maintenant j'écris un livre sur le vol de nuit. Mais dans son sens intime c'est un livre sur la nuit. (Je n'ai jamais vécu qu'après neuf heures du soir).
>
> Voilà le début, c'est les premiers souvenirs sur la nuit: "Nous rêvions dans le vestibule quand tombait la nuit. Nous guettions le passage des lampes: on les portait comme une charge de fleurs et chacune remuait au mur des ombres belles comme des palmes. Puis le mirage tournait, puis on enfermait au salon ce bouquet de lumière et de palmes sombres. Alors, le jour était fini pour nous et, dans nos lits d'enfants, on nous embarquait vers un autre jour. Ma mère, vous vous penchiez sur nous, sur ce départ d'anges et pour que le voyage soit possible, pour que rien n'agitât nos rêves, vous effaciez du drap ce pli, cette ombre, cette houle... Car on apaise un lit comme d'un doigt divin la mer." Ensuite ce sont des traversées de la nuit moins protégées, l'avion.

In the event, Saint-Exupéry decided not to open *Vol de nuit* in this way, yet these memories of childhood not only surface in the scene between the European mail-pilot and his wife, but haunt the novel indirectly. This whole sense of childhood as a lamp-lit sanctuary presided over by maternal solicitude and love seems to me to explain the emotional weight that attaches to the contrasts, persistently made in this novel, between light and dark, repose and agitation, security and danger. Another childhood memory suggests, even more precisely, the particular resonances that are associated with night flying in the novel. As a child, Antoine read Jules Verne's *Les Indes noires*,[3] and its revelation on the subterranean world of the miner picking his way through the darkness with the aid of a small lamp helps to fix for us the full significance of the recurring images of 'plumbing the darkness' which we get in *Vol de nuit* and which I intend to explore in detail in chapter 5. Essentially, the child's fear of

---

[3] 'Books I remember', *Harper's Bazaar* (April 1941), 82 and 123.

the darkness is displaced on to the adult's determination to
brave and conquer the surrounding night. In the same way,
the feelings of comfort and relief linked to the lamplight of
childhood are transposed into the lonely pilot's grateful
response to the glimmer of stars, the glow of his instrument
panel, and the lamps of distant townships.

So far, I have tended to stress the high density of autobiographical detail that enters into *Vol de nuit* and to show how
these details are modified in the service of a central story. By
a natural transition, this leads me to examine the specifically
fictional conventions which are present in the text. First, it is
worth recalling that the text of some 150 pages which
Gallimard published in 1931 was reduced from a much larger
original manuscript of 400 pages (*1*, p. 230). We may assume
that in so radical a pruning exercise something of interest and
value had to go. I suspect that a number of fictional or
'invented' developments were sacrificed and, as a result, *Vol
de nuit* emerges as rather too abstract, as being deficient in
what has been called the 'thick texture of life' – at least, once
we get away from the intensely rendered struggles in the air.
The decision to reduce the original manuscript has certainly
produced a text notable for its concentration and economy,
and I think it has done so in order to throw into high relief
the creed of duty which is given explicit expression in the
words of Rivière. I shall return to this, in chapter 3, when I
look closely at Rivière's observations, but here I am anxious
only to make the point that the pared-down structure of *Vol
de nuit* serves a didactic purpose.

That purpose is fundamentally unsympathetic to fictional
excursions, to anything that is extraneous to the ideas being
put forward. We can see this bias at work in the relative
absence of concrete details about characters and in the limited
degree of curiosity which the narrator displays toward them.
Admittedly, a few fictionalised excursions do go beyond the
strict needs of the primary plot which is about Fabien's
struggle and fate in the skies. I think, in particular, about the
revelations involving Robineau's private life, and about the
marital scene between the pilot scheduled for the European
run and his wife. Yet, most of the time, as I hope to show in

chapter 4, character tends to remain only thinly explored. The episodic narrative structure of *Vol de nuit* actually reinforces this tendency. The action, which alternates between plane and ground control, between open sky and the enclosed spaces of town or company office or private room, is articulated through twenty-three short chapters, some only three or four pages long. The rapid, and occasionally abrupt, transitions from chapter to chapter certainly create a strong sense of forward momentum but they also tend to fragment experience and to 'flatten' character because they allow so little time for elaboration.

These constant shifts might be judged to weaken fatally the unity of the narrative. Such is not the case. It is successfully held together by a single omniscient narrator and by a simple basic plot – the progress of Fabien's doomed flight – to which the sub-plots involving Rivière's vigil and the activities of Fabien's wife are clearly related. The narrative is also contained within a strict temporal framework: everything occurs within about twenty-four hours. The general result is to produce a narrative that is effectively unified. It might be said that excursions like that into Robineau's apartment or into the bedroom of the pilot about to set off for Europe, are insufficiently filled out to make them truly interesting as fiction and, in this respect, distract needlessly from the main thrust of the narrative. However, I would want to say that such excursions represent an integral part of the pattern of alternating action and reflection, tension and relaxation, embodied in the arrangement of the chapters.

( i i )

*Vol de nuit* was written (1930) close to the experiences on which it draws and, one feels, while still under their spell. The same sense of immediacy does not characterise *Terre des hommes*. In fact, it incorporates a number of texts that had previously appeared elsewhere and these give the impression of having been put together to make up a book. To turn from *Vol de nuit* to the pages of *Terre des hommes* is to move from a text that is basically fictional, even if embedded in the author's real-life experience, to a quite different kind of text in which autobiography, in the form of scattered recollections, predominates. Such recollections prompt, and are framed by, a series of reflections on man's moral and spiritual needs and aspirations. What chiefly strikes one about these reflections is that they are developed more fully and in a much more discursive way than occurs in *Vol de nuit.* In a word, they impress one as discrete entities, unlike *Vol de nuit* where the reflections are integrated, with a large measure of success, into one central, unfolding action. So, in spite of their common roots in Saint-Exupéry's personal experiences as a flier, *Vol de nuit* and *Terre des hommes* differ greatly in their form and rhythms.

The twenty-three compact chapters of *Vol de nuit,* following rapidly on one another, and often alive with the energy of their immediacy, are replaced by a more leisurely and spacious narrative pattern of eight chapters, usually much longer than those of *Vol de nuit,* though chapters VI, VII and VIII are sub-divided into a number of sections. Paradoxically, this new arrangement of the material, though it achieves a more static overall effect than is the case with *Vol de nuit,* does little to remove our sense of the episodic nature of the work. As we move from one crash or ordeal to the next, from one protagonist to another, from one geographical location to another, and from one point in the past to another, our perception of the general unity of *Terre des hommes* is greatly weakened, at least at the level of narrative. This impression is reinforced by the way in which narrated action is constantly interwoven with passages of philosophic reflection. It is difficult not to feel that materials of varying kinds have been assembled rather opportunistically and juxtaposed in a loose way that does not reflect the inevitable-seeming order which successful works of the imagination normally display. This does not mean that the ordering of this text is in any sense random but simply that, unlike a novel or play, it is not shaped so as to lead to an invented and persuasive end.

In drawing even more extensively on Saint-Exupéry's personal experience as a flier, *Terre des hommes* no longer bothers to conceal the protagonist under invented names. The autobiographical incidents are presented to us as such, though Saint-Exupéry does not follow a strict chronological sequence in narrating these events. After a reflective introduction ('La terre nous en apprend plus long sur nous que tous les livres'), he begins at the beginning by recalling his early days as a trainee pilot at Toulouse in 1926: the jolting ride to the airfield in a rickety bus and the take-off at dawn. There follows, in the normal chronological order, an episode dating from May 1930 in which Mermoz is caught up in a cyclone in the South Atlantic and sees great waterspouts below him like 'les piliers noirs d'un temple'. Then the narrative reverts to an earlier incident which took place in 1927 when Saint-Exupéry and his radio-operator made a navigational error when on a flight to Villa Cisneros (now Dakhla) in North Africa. A break in the narrative now occurs as Saint-Exupéry recalls the career and tragic death of Mermoz in 1936. The narrative proper then resumes with an account of a forced landing in the desert which took place in 1927 and which involved Saint-Exupéry and a handful of other pilots and mechanics in building a makeshift encampment of wooden crates so as to protect themselves against marauding tribesmen. By a natural transition, the narrative then moves forward to another, more punishing ordeal, when Guillaumet came down in the Andes in 1930 and emerged alive after an heroic struggle. This prompts the narrator to recall an unspecified forced landing in the desert and the sense of wonder it engendered in him, in the face of the silent planet at night. This in turn sparks off his recollections of the old housekeeper in his childhood home. By association with these childhood memories, the narrative then jumps forward in time and Saint-Exupéry recalls a stop-over he made near Concordia in Argentina (presumably during his tour of duty there in 1929-30) when he was given hospitality at a rambling and dilapidated old house in the country.

The next stage in the narrative occurs when the narrator goes back in time to an episode which took place in February 1927. This involves a forced landing on the Río de Oro coastline which resulted in Saint-Exupéry spending the night

at a small fort near Nouakchott, the present-day capital of
Mauretania. This incident had already been exploited in
Saint-Exupéry's first novel, *Courrier sud* (1929). Picking up
the normal chronological sequence, the narrator now gives an
account of his relations with the slave Bark during the period
1927-28 when he was in charge of the airfield at Fort Juby.
The next significant moment in the narrative comes when
Saint-Exupéry recounts graphically his crash-landing and
desperate ordeal in the Libyan desert (end of December
1935). Simultaneously, we are given a couple of brief flash-
backs to Guillaumet's ordeal in the Andes in June 1930. The
desert ordeal gives rise to an extended interlude of philosophic reflection before the narrative proper moves to its
conclusion with Saint-Exupéry's account of his experiences
as a special correspondent during the Spanish Civil War
(August 1936 and June-July 1937).

If I have gone into some detail about the narrative ordering of the text, it is to emphasise that it does not offer a
simple linear progression. The temporal shifts reinforce our
sense of the constant intertraffic between past and present in
human life. The past regularly infiltrates and colours the
narrator's present and helps to determine its significance.
More than that, these remembered moments of high excitement, great tension or exhausting ordeal are framed by
philosophic interludes which they both feed and illustrate.
The selection and ordering of these autobiographical episodes
serve a purpose beyond them, that of finding significance in
the welter of past experience and of making experience yield
what might be called a philosophy of life. This alternation of
vivid and concrete incidents from the past with passages of
sober reflection certainly suggests a kind of unifying pattern
in the text, but ultimately, the unity of *Terre des hommes*
derives principally from its recurring moral and philosophical themes.

*Vol de nuit* is deficient in pure invention; *Terre des
hommes* has almost none though, in the arrangement of its
autobiographical materials, it does contrive to produce a
sense of formal structure. It could be said that the story of
Bark goes furthest in the direction of filling out the text with

fictional possibilities but, if so, it is an exception and does not bulk large when set against the many pieces that are drawn directly from Saint-Exupéry's earlier reportages. Just how directly it would be tedious to show in detail. What is generally true is that the process through which Saint-Exupéry transposes his own lived experience into the fiction of *Vol de nuit* – exploiting a variety of literary devices, including a high density of metaphor and simile and a pattern of alternating tension and relaxation – has no exact counterpart in the way in which he transfers his original journalism into the finished text of *Terre des hommes*. But then, it is worth remembering that Saint-Exupéry's original newspaper reports already display a high degree of literary expressiveness. Similarly, they are already in the process of re-creating the observed world in terms of the writer's constant preoccupation with man's dignity, responsibility and need to surpass the limits of his everyday self. It still has to be said that Saint-Exupéry's newspaper texts are often transferred to *Terre des hommes* with only minimal changes. To take one example: the tenderly-written scene of the sergeant waking from sleep in war-torn Madrid (*TH,* pp. 163-65) faithfully reproduces the same scene as reported in the articles he wrote for *Paris-Soir* in June and July 1937.[4] Similarly, the vivid account of his crash in the Libyan desert given to the newspaper *L'Intransigeant* (January-February 1936) is repeated almost word for word in the English text of *Wind, Sand and Stars* and reappears in slightly condensed form in *Terre des hommes.*

The essential point I am trying to make here is that the fictive elements which help to transform the autobiographical experiences underlying *Vol de nuit* are hardly present at all in *Terre des hommes,* though Saint-Exupéry is just as much concerned in the latter text to create a meaningful pattern out of the plethora of incidents which he describes. *Vol de nuit* and *Terre des hommes* inhabit the same moral universe and concerned share the same sensibility, but the element of fiction in the latter survives only in residual form through the

---

[4] Reprinted in *Un Sens à la vie* (Paris, Gallimard, 1956), 133-36.

unifying narrative voice, the persistent underlying effort to
raise the exploits of the fliers to the level of a modern epic,
and, in a limited way, through the narrator's attempts to enter
imaginatively into the inner life of Bark and to conjure up the
texture of an alien world. However, such attempts tend to be
disappointingly conventional, as in the following passage:
'Bark écoutait chanter l'eau des fontaines, là où nulle fontaine ne coula jamais. Et Bark, les yeux fermés, croyait
habiter une maison blanche, assise chaque nuit sous la même
étoile, là où les hommes habitent des maisons de bure et
poursuivent le vent' (*TH,* p. 101).

In *Terre des hommes* all is recollection. The past has been
retrieved, reordered, but it is not imaginatively transformed.
Yet, in spite of the much higher incidence of discursive
writing in this text, *story-telling* is central to it, as it is to *Vol
de nuit.* It is ultimately through stories that both seek to elicit
meaning from human experience. In this respect, it is wholly
revealing that when Saint-Exupéry is at his lowest ebb in the
Libyan desert, he recalls the seductive appeal of the fictions
he invents during the moments of near-delirium brought on
by thirst and exhaustion: 'Cela me peine de finir par le froid.
Je préférerais mes mirages intérieurs. Cette croix, ces Arabes,
ces lampes. Après tout, cela commençait à m'intéresser' (*TH,*
p. 148).

# 2

# Man, Plane and Planet

I N using 'man' exclusively in the title of this and the two
following chapters, I want deliberately to underline the degree to which the world of *Vol de nuit* and *Terre des hommes*
is a narrowly male world, and in some parts of what follows, I
hope to tease out the full implications of this maleness. First,
however, I want to concentrate on the novelty of the perspective which Saint-Exupéry's picture of flying affords us. Part
of Saint-Exupéry's talent as a writer certainly lies in his skill
at conveying graphically what it is like to negotiate the
constantly changing skies. He is particularly deft at showing
the complexity of the activity of flying: its combination of
speed, practical skills, mental alertness and vivid apprehen-
sion of natural forces, together with its moments of exhilara-
tion and fear. He successfully unifies these discrete elements
in a dramatic fusion which powerfully involves the reader.
Over and above this, one meets in *Vol de nuit* and *Terre des
hommes,* in a fresh and original way, a more specific set of
insights that previous literature of the air has tended to
neglect or to explore perfunctorily. I am referring here to the
way in which Saint-Exupéry throws into high relief the fact
that the plane is both a tool and an extension of the human
person who operates it. He is especially good at showing how,
in the act of flying, man and plane become one.

As our author was to say in a piece he wrote about test
pilots in August 1939: 'l'avion n'est pas seulement une
collection de paramètres, mais un organisme que l'on aus-
culte'.[5] Saint-Exupéry fills out this idea imaginatively in *Vol*

[5] As reprinted in René Delange, *La Vie de Saint-Exupéry* (Paris, Seuil,
1948), Appendix II, 215.

*de nuit.* We have only to recall Fabien flying up from Patagonia. Absorbed in reading the dials on his instrument panel, he becomes part of a single living entity: '[il] sentit dans le métal ruisseler la vie: le métal ne vibrait pas, mais vivait. Les cinq cents chevaux du moteur faisaient naître dans la matière un courant très doux, qui changeait sa glace en chair de velours. Une fois de plus, le pilote n'éprouvait, en vol, ni vertige, ni ivresse, mais le travail mystérieux d'une chair vivante' (*VN*, pp. 21-22). It is part of Saint-Exupéry's distinction as a writer that he makes it possible for his non-flying reader to share this fresh insight into the nature of flying, an insight he expands in more discursive terms in *Terre des hommes*. In this text he argues that, as the machine becomes perfected, we cease to be aware of it as a machine – 'la machine se dissimule' (*TH*, p. 52). The consequences for the operator are very significant: 'Cette attention n'est plus absorbée par l'outil. Au-delà de l'outil, et à travers lui, c'est la vieille nature que nous retrouvons, celle du jardinier, du navigateur, ou du poète' (p. 52).

Two things need to be said about this. First, it confirms the degree to which agent and instrument are identified in the act of flying, and secondly, it implies that the instrument has become a means of revealing the world in a new light. This tool may be likened by Saint-Exupéry to a plough (*TH*, p. 49) but its effects are more momentous. It abolishes all our received ideas of space and time: 'Les notions de séparation, d'absence, de distance, de retour... ne contiennent plus les mêmes réalités' (*TH*, p. 50). *Vol de nuit* and *Terre des hommes* are certainly about strange and faraway places which, at the time Saint-Exupéry wrote of them, were unknown to most of his readers, but the main interest of these texts does not lie in their local colour or exoticism. The earth, seen from the vantage point of the pilot working for a pioneering airline, does not present itself simply as a colourful and variegated show, in the manner of travel literature. In fact, as Saint-Exupéry vividly depicts it, the plane not only reveals our planet in a wholly new perspective which modifies our relationship to the familiar world, but it permits us to discover fresh insights into our own natures. The experience of pilot and plane may be dramatically revealed as one of mutual dependence but this points to the larger dependence of human beings on their fellows and on the planet they inhabit. Indeed, the prominence given in both texts to the imperative need to create bonds between human beings and between them and the planet which is their natural habitat, emerges as one of the persistent and distinctive themes of Saint-Exupéry's writing.

In *Terre des hommes* Saint-Exupéry pays homage to the power of the elements by granting them mythical status: 'trois divinités élémentaires, la montagne, la mer et l'orage' (p. 30). The elements are indeed dangerous, a threat to human life, and they have to be grappled with and overcome. Yet the flier is not seen as a solitary and self-conscious agent alienated from the natural world. In a very concrete sense, the earth is seen to be the airman's home. The solitude and freedom of flying may bring out the contemplative side of his nature, making him especially attentive to his own identity, but they also bring him an altered consciousness of his relationship to the planet. This rediscovery of the 'real' nature of our planet and of the aviator's place in it comes about precisely through his active grappling with obstacles, dangers and the threat of death. The plane reduces the gap between the pilot and the earth. It acts as a sort of conduit through which he learns to know the world, to achieve a new awareness of the way in which he belongs to it, and to gain a fresh perspective on the nature and beauties of that earth, quite different from his earth-bound experience of it. As Saint-Exupéry puts it in *Terre des hommes*: 'L'avion est une machine sans doute, mais quel instrument d'analyse! Cet instrument nous a fait découvrir le vrai visage de la terre' (p. 54).

Quite simply, the earth viewed from the flier's vertical perspective is disposed about him spatially in a radically different way. Just as the peasant tilling the soil comes up against the earth's resistance to human effort, so the flier discovers the world below him as a series of landmarks to be noted and obstacles to be overcome; in other words, as a system of necessary limits and constraints. In this sense, the world is ordered in accordance with the needs and desires of

the human agent who lives on it. It does not offer itself to the
pilot as pure spectacle but as a network of possibilities
through which his creative will can work. Let us look at how
these themes and insights are given concrete expression in
*Vol de nuit* and *Terre des hommes*.

The idea of the aircraft as a tool is implied in *Vol de nuit*
but given prominence only in *Terre des hommes*, and this
very fact tends to confirm the deliberately philosophical
dimension in the latter. The idea springs from a series of
observations which appear early on in the text and which,
typically for Saint-Exupéry, offer the labour of the peasant
as a model for creative human effort. He begins with a
revealing aphorism: 'La terre nous en apprend plus long sur
nous que tous les livres. Parce qu'elle nous résiste' (*TH*, p. 9).
He expands this point by arguing that, like the peasant in his
struggle with the soil, man learns about nature and discovers
the meaning of existence through the implements he uses. He
concludes: 'De même l'avion, l'outil des lignes aériennes,
mêle l'homme à tous les vieux problèmes' (p. 9). There
follows, spread out through the text of *Terre des hommes*, a
series of incidents which illustrate concretely from Saint-
Exupéry's own experience the precise nature of this instrumental link between plane and planet.

Saint-Exupéry recalls, in his apprentice days as a flier,
poring over a map with the veteran flier Guillaumet and
entering with him into the world of instrumentality and
practicality. The map is one thing, Guillaumet's exact indica-
tions of the hazards offered by certain topographical features,
quite another. These three orange trees, growing in a part of
the terrain over which the mail-plane has to pass, are not
objects of natural beauty but a hazard to pilots. Similarly, this
stream which appears to feed a\fertile meadow is not what it
seems. It forms an area of marshy ground at the edge of a
landing strip and has to be avoided. In the receptive imagination of the young pilot this fertile spot becomes a place of
potential dread, where his aircraft could suddenly crash and
be transformed 'en gerbe de flammes...' (*TH*, p. 16). This
sense of the earth viewed instrumentally, in the light of the
pilot's needs and goals, is also conveyed by a dramatic little

episode in which Saint-Exupéry and his radio-operator mistake a star for the light of the control tower at Villa Cisneros and find themselves flying off course: 'Ainsi les nécessités qu'impose un métier, transforment et enrichissent le monde. Il n'est même point besoin de nuit semblable pour faire découvrir par le pilote de ligne un sens nouveau aux vieux spectacles. Le paysage monotone, qui fatigue le passager, est déjà autre pour l'équipage. Cette masse nuageuse, qui barre l'horizon, cesse pour lui d'être un décor: elle intéressera ses muscles et lui posera des problèmes' (*TH,* p. 29). A subsequent passage reinforces this point in an extended, and characteristic, simile in which the pilot is likened to the peasant inspecting his fields: 'Ces couleurs de la terre et du ciel, ces traces de vent sur la mer, ces nuages dorés du crépuscule, il ne les admire point, mais les médite. Semblable au paysan qui fait sa tournée dans son domaine et qui prévoit, à mille signes, la marche du printemps, la menace du gel, l'annonce de la pluie, le pilote de métier, lui aussi, déchiffre des signes de neige, des signes de brume, des signes de nuit bienheureuse' (*TH,* p. 30).

In all these examples Saint-Exupéry brings home to us, in a memorable way, a valuable insight that will later be exploited by thinkers like Sartre: the world is always to be seen in the light of what human will and imagination propose to do with it. How we see it is inseparable from the intentions we have for it. It is this, essentially philosophical, insight which Saint-Exupéry uncovers in imaginative terms and enables us to share. And this world, saturated, as it were, with human intentions, is brought alive for us in one of the most brilliant descriptive passages of *Vol de nuit.* It is that passage in which the pilot, flying the mail-plane down from Paraguay, approaches the city of Buenos Aires (*VN,* pp. 181-82). Everything here – the description of the terrain speeding below as a flower-filled garden, the twinkling lights of the town seen as an opulent display of precious stones and metals, the image of Buenos Aires itself as a treasure-trove soon to be attained, the final musical figure of a joyful sonata – conspires to show the earth not in some objective or quasi-scientific way but as suffused with the relief, pleasure and anticipation that emanate from the pilot who observes it and who has brought the mail successfully to its destination, to a great settlement that is the handiwork of man, after a long travail in the clouds.

Yet the very emphasis in *Vol de nuit* on an alluring and brilliantly lit Buenos Aires as the 'home' to which the tired aviator is irresistibly drawn, leads to a seeming paradox that is made explicit in *Terre des hommes*. On the one hand, the earth is man's natural home. It offers him the basic conditions and materials from which to create a human order. On the other hand, this planet, though it exerts a powerful pull on man, both gravitational and in terms of human need for a secure settlement that can protect and sustain life, is frequently pictured by Saint-Exupéry as forbidding and inhospitable. Seen from the skies, themselves a cockpit of warring elements, the face of the planet below is characterised by hard, bare and inhuman places: rock-strewn wastes, mountains, burning deserts. This paradox is more apparent than real, as the pages of *Terre des hommes* make plain. Essentially, the earth's obstacles and dangers constitute the necessary challenge to human energy, endurance, courage and inventiveness. Without such a challenge, Saint-Exupéry implies, there can be no creative human response. Hence, the earth as man's natural home and the earth as hostile environment are simply two sides of the same coin. The challenge of what is difficult is necessary if man is to realise his full potential.

These insights find expression in some of the most striking pages of *Terre des hommes*. I recall, for example, that meditative passage in which the narrator describes how the harsh reality of the earth's foundations is disclosed to the aviator: 'le soubassement essentiel, l'assise de rocs, de sable, et de sel, où la vie, quelquefois, comme un peu de mousse au creux des ruines, ici et là se hasarde à fleurir. Nous voilà donc changés en physiciens, en biologistes... Nous voilà donc jugeant l'homme à l'échelle cosmique' (*TH*, p. 55). What is significant here is that the accumulation of the images of sterility (rock, sand, ruins) does not exclude the possibility of the germination of life. And his sense of life surviving in spite of an unpropitious environment is carried over into a later passage, though it is now linked with the nurturing skills of human beings. The airman flying south of Río Gallegos passes over a landscape of petrified lava that very gradually gives way to vegetation, sparse at first but more luxuriant as he gets near to Punta Arenas. There the grudging terrain shows the results of human labour, 'ces jardins préparés', and this prompts Saint-Exupéry to write: 'si près des coulées noires, comme on sent bien le miracle de l'homme!' (p. 57), a miracle accomplished against a resisting earth. The author's explicit praise for this 'human miracle' and the hopefulness it implies, does not prevent his returning, later in the text, to a kind of appalled recognition of how much of the planet is arid waste: 'Dieu que cette planète est donc déserte!... Quelle part de roc et de sable!' (pp. 112-13).

This 'instrumental' view of our planet, which Saint-Exupéry's picture does so much to capture and make actual to us, has an important aspect – important, that is, for the kind of humanism he tries to formulate and which I intend examining in detail in the next chapter. This aspect involves a powerful fascination with landscape seen as the embodiment of permanence and continuity. We can see this fascination at work in a number of passages. There is, for example, a moment in *Terre des hommes* when the author/narrator recalls looking down on a series of cone-shaped hills with flat tops, standing in the Sahara desert. These are compared to pillars which testify to the 'vaste plateau qui les unissait autrefois' (p. 59). In a similar vein, Saint-Exupéry recollects the thrill of landing on territory 'que nul jamais encore, bête ou homme, n'avait souillé' and discovering 'un sable infiniment vierge' (p. 60). He concludes: 'J'étais le premier à faire ruisseler, d'une main dans l'autre, comme un or précieux, cette poussière de coquillages. Le premier à troubler ce silence. Sur cette sorte de banquise polaire qui, de toute éternité, n'avait pas formé un seul brin d'herbe, j'étais, comme une semence apportée par les vents, le premier témoignage de la vie' (pp. 60-61). Two emotions characteristic of the airman's world in Saint-Exupéry are in evidence here. The first is a sort of awe before the age of the world, before enduring natural phenomena that dwarf and outlast

man. The second is the thrill of pride that comes from
recognising the power of human consciousness to stand apart
from this inert natural world and to make sense of its
fragmentary evidence. This is even more clearly the case
when the narrator identifies the black, shining detritus that
lies around him – 'lourd comme du métal, et coulé en forme
de larme' (p. 61) – as meteors that have fallen from the sky
æons ago.

Saint-Exupéry's fascination with the primordial, with the
durability of the earth in time and space, is inseparable from
his preoccupation with *human* continuity, with his need to be
assured of a permanent home for mankind. Nothing reflects
this more sharply than another episode in which the author/
narrator of *Terre des hommes* is involved. He has been
forced down in the desert at night and falls asleep. On
waking, he looks up, is made dizzy by the teeming stars
above, as though he were in free fall with nothing to hang on
to. Then suddenly he becomes aware of the earth's gravitational pull under him, a force he likens to the 'sovereign'
power of love (p. 63). He is 'riveted' to the earth and his
shoulders seem 'in harmony' with the weight they feel. This
image conveys graphically the idea of this planet being man's
natural home, a kind of counterweight to the frightening
boundlessness of space. Such an insight gains its strength
from knowing as an airman what it is like to be adrift in space
and to have one's old familiar relationship with the earth
radically altered.

The desert, like the sea (with which Saint-Exupéry often
compares it), is peculiarly expressive of the primordial character of the earth, and it represents the central image of *Terre
des hommes* – one has only to think of how large chapter VI
('Dans le désert') and chapter VII ('Au centre du désert') bulk
in the narrative. Both chapters convey brilliantly the desert's
sterile emptiness, its heat and silence, the glacial beauty of
its nights. Both suggest powerfully how hostile this terrain
appears to human life. This hostility is sometimes expressed
through an accumulation of naturalistic detail, as when Saint-
Exupéry is cast adrift in the desert after his crash: 'Je me lève
et je marche. Mais bientôt je suis pris d'un insupportable

tremblement. Mon sang déshydraté circule très mal, et un froid glacial me pénètre, qui n'est pas seulement le froid de la nuit. Mes mâchoires claquent et tout mon corps est agité de soubresauts' (p. 147). But it is depicted even more graphically in a passage in which the transient and mortal narrator is confronted with the detritus of the ages, in the shape of a petrified forest: 'Une forêt antédiluvienne jonche le sol de ses fûts brisés. Elle s'est écroulée comme une cathédrale, voilà cent mille ans, sous un ouragan de genèse' (p. 135).

This passage exemplifies how the 'eternity' of the desert provokes human bewilderment and despair while, elsewhere in the text, the spectacle of the agelessness of the earth affords the human observer something close to solace because it seems to guarantee a permanent home for man. The timeless desert can indeed appear not simply to outlast man but to mock him, but this does not represent the whole of Saint-Exupéry's conception of the desert. Significantly he also suggests the possibility of a kind of creative tension between it and man. This is not only evidenced by the success with which the airline manages to operate in these highly unfavourable climatic conditions, but it is even present in the ordeal of Prévot and Saint-Exupéry. Through the savage trials of heat and thirst, they are tested, find enhanced knowledge of themselves, and in surpassing their normal limits, affirm their full humanity. Elsewhere the idea of men learning to understand and cope with the desert as a part, though a very exacting part, of their natural habitat, is given prominence. For example, the airman flying over the desert is constantly alert to wells and oases, and determines for himself the viability of the desert in the light of his own needs and goals. As Saint-Exupéry states it: 'Le Sahara, c'est en nous qu'il se montre' (*TH,* p. 77).

Connected with this is the notion of man entering into co-operation with the desert, once he has learned to understand it. Saint-Exupéry illustrates this idea by two sharply etched sketches. In the first, he leaves his wrecked plane and sets out across the sand in search of water and help. He stumbles on the tracks of a desert fox (*le fénech*) and discovers that it feeds off snails that live on the rare, stunted bushes that grow around. Gradually he finds out that the fox, by limiting his ration of snails from each bush, prudently avoids exhausting this precious source of food: 'Tout ce passe comme s'il avait la conscience du risque. S'il se rassasiait sans précaution, il n'y aurait plus d'escargots. S'il n'y avait point d'escargots, il n'y aurait point de fénechs' (p. 134). There is a lesson here for man. He too can learn to survive in the earth's unpropitious places if, like the desert fox, he adapts to the terrain, calls on his endurance and ingenuity, and respects the earth's ecology.

The second illustration of man's capacity for making something positive out of an implacable natural setting occurs when the author/narrator finds himself in the desert at Port-Etienne (now Nouadhibou in Mauretania). He is preparing for a night flight. The night is calm and clear, and suddenly a green butterfly and two dragonflies emerge from the dusk and flutter around his lamp. Their presence in this place is evidence that a sandstorm is blowing far out in the desert and so the pilot is warned of what to expect. Here Saint-Exupéry is shown reading nature like a code, and the implication is that natural phenomena, properly interpreted, can come to man's aid. The narrator is filled with delight 'd'avoir compris à demi-mot un langage secret' (*TH*, p. 84). The incident epitomises the way in which the human and natural worlds are connected: we have our place in the natural order but we have to learn to interpret it correctly and to respect it.

The moral lessons that are implicit in these two incidents point to the figurative or symbolic dimension that is often present in *Vol de nuit* and *Terre des hommes*. So it is not surprising to find that the desert is not simply *locus*, a specific geographical location where the movements of nomadic tribes occur, but also *topos*, a place symbolic of timelessness and permanence and of man's struggle to establish a distinctively human and spiritual order in the world. In Saint-Exupéry's hands, it becomes a magical and secret kingdom, very like the country-house garden of his childhood, a garden invested with meaning and potency through the imagination of the children who play in it. In a comparable way, the desert is where man's dreams of self-realisation can be played out and where 'les seules richesses véritables' (*TH, p.* 94) are to be discovered. In this respect, Saint-Exupéry seems to echo, whether consciously or not, one of Nietzsche's aphorisms in *Thus Spoke Zarathustra,* a text he was familiar with from his student days: 'But in the loneliest desert the second metamorphosis occurs: the spirit here becomes a lion; it wants to capture freedom and be lord in its own desert' (*4,* p. 54).

Throughout this chapter I have tried to trace a series of connections which seem to me important for our understanding of Saint-Exupéry's fundamental vision of life in *Vol de nuit* and *Terre des hommes.* Starting with the notion of the plane as tool and an extension of the pilot who operates it, Saint-Exupéry introduces us to a new perspective on our planet, a perspective whose novelty was, of course, much greater when his books first appeared. Indeed, this new angle on the earth is inseparable from the kind of flying in which the pioneer airmen were involved. In this respect, Saint-Exupéry is typical of them, but he is not typical in the insights he derives from this experience. It is through his exceptional vision that the earth is revealed to us as readers in all its agelessness and stubborn materiality, but also as man's natural home, a challenge to his creative powers and his capacity to endure. On this planet, the desert is singled out as the ultimate proving-ground of man and as the symbol of his restless search to realise himself fully, to establish links between men, and so to create a viable human order in the world.

**3**

# The Vocation of Man

T H E awe expressed in both *Vol de nuit* and *Terre des hommes* before the spectacle of nature, before mountains, rocks and deserts which have withstood the attrition of time and which testify to the earth's continuity and permanence, seems to fire Saint-Exupéry's ambition to create an enduring monument that will rival the agelessness of our natural setting. This tradition of humanism is fundamentally optimistic, quite at variance with the sense of the futility of human effort when measured against the erosion of time and nature which we encounter in a Romantic poem like Shelley's 'Ozymandias', where the huge effigy of a long-dead king lies shattered in the desert: 'Nothing beside remains. Round the decay / Of that colossal wreck, boundless and bare / The lone and level sands stretch far away'. For Saint-Exupéry, however, the belief that a lasting cultural and spiritual monument can be achieved by man is central to his writing, but so is his conviction that it can be created only if man surpasses his workaday self and realises what is finest in him. This implies that there is an innate nobility in human beings that needs to be brought out. In this sense, the true vocation of man is to go beyond his normal limits. What exactly is the character of this humanistic creed as restated by Saint-Exupéry for the twentieth century? How is it developed in the two texts under discussion and how persuasive is it?

In his original preface to *Vol de nuit,* Gide not only sees the novel as a hymn to the acts and sacrifices of the pioneers of flying but as a memorial to a vanishing age. Already he contrasts the disinterested and benign courage of these pilots with the technological and chemical warfare that is to come (p. 12). Gide and Saint-Exupéry were rapidly overtaken by events. The malign power of the plane was soon to be seen at work in the destruction of unarmed villagers by Italian bombers in Ethiopia in 1935 and by the cruel bombardment of the small Basque town of Guernica in April 1937 during the Spanish Civil War. Hence, the unique value of *Vol de nuit* and *Terre des hommes* lies in recapturing imaginatively that heroic phase of the 1920s and 1930s when commercial flying could still be thought of as a high adventure, uncontaminated by sectarian passion and sustained by the fraternity of like-minded fellow pilots. It is only by isolating and concentrating on this kind of flying that Saint-Exupéry can invent the conditions necessary to produce his moral philosophy.

Behind the insistence on the joys and demands of one's craft as an aviator, behind the exceptional moral status which Saint-Exupéry tends to grant to commercial flying in *Vol de nuit* and *Terre des hommes,* there lurks a kind of nostalgia for a simpler world, perhaps a pre-industrial world, in which the skills and dedication of craftsmen themselves represent a morally satisfying way of life. In order to throw his preferred values into relief, Saint-Exupéry tends to do two things. First, in concentrating on the skills of hand and eye, especially in the more graphic passages of *Vol de nuit,* he paradoxically abstracts the activity of flying from the world of sophisticated technology to which it properly belongs. For if, in those heady moments in the air, the plane can be said to liberate man from the tyranny of distance and gravity, it also represents a symptom of that industrialism of the production-line which enslaves man. In Saint-Exupéry's hands, this negative aspect of the technological process, in which the airman is necessarily inserted, is played down in order that we can focus on the mastery of skills displayed by the exceptional individual. So, though in *Vol de nuit* the narrator itemises, in documentary fashion, the technical equipment of the plane – 'Il tapota le tableau de distribution électrique, toucha les contacts un à un... poussa en place sa lampe de secours... la quitta de nouveau pour tapoter chaque manette... se permit d'allumer une lampe, d'orner sa carlingue d'instruments précis, et surveilla sur les cadrans seuls, son entrée dans la nuit'

(p. 22) – elsewhere he tends to neutralise this mechanical picture by likening the plane to a plough.

This comparison, which he makes explicitly in an interview he gave in 1939, is peculiarly significant of Saint-Exupéry's world-view: 'Il n'y a qu'une seule vérité pour le pilote et le jardinier. La machine n'est pas un but. C'est un outil. Un outil comme la charrue'.[6] This brings us to Saint-Exupéry's second tendency, that of connecting the pilot and his skills with the rural world of craftsmen and peasants. Such a view recurs frequently in both *Vol de nuit* and *Terre des hommes*. In the former, the airman Fabien is described as 'le berger des petites villes' (*VN*, p. 18), while the pilot who puts on his flying gear before setting out on the European run is likened to a peasant: 'il s'habillait comme un paysan' (p. 96). Elsewhere, the pilot of the Asunción mail is depicted as a goatherd: 'les yeux grands ouverts et pleins de lune' (p. 182). For his part, Pellerin speaks of his flying experiences in the plain idiom of an honest craftsman: 'parler de son vol comme un forgeron de son enclume' (p. 42). The same imagery is exploited in *Terre des hommes*. The author/narrator refers to himself as a 'paysan des escales' (*TH*, p. 150), while Mermoz's pioneering flights conjure up the doughty tiller of the soil: 'Ainsi Mermoz avait défriché les sables, la montagne, la nuit et la mer' (*TH*, p. 33). When he dies prematurely in the course of a flight, he is compared to '[le] moissonneur qui, ayant bien lié sa gerbe, se couche dans son champ' (p. 34). These constant references to the life of the countryside are linked with Saint-Exupéry's implied or explicit preference for a certain set of values. Rural society is seen as an organic community and is identified with nurture and creativity, and with order, patriarchal authority, and stability. Such a view of the world is summed up in certain passages of *Terre des hommes*. I think particularly of the author's evocation of the death of the old peasant: 'Elle est si douce quand elle est dans l'ordre des choses, quand le vieux paysan de Provence, au terme de son règne, remet en dépôt à ses fils son lot de

[6] Jacques Baratier, 'Retour d'Amérique, Saint-Exupéry nous dit...', *Les Nouvelles Littéraires* (18 March 1939).

chèvres et d'oliviers, afin qu'ils le transmettent, à leur tour, aux fils de leurs fils. On ne meurt qu'à demi dans une lignée paysanne' (*TH*, p. 176).

One can appreciate the hankering for immortality concealed in this passage, but there is something disconcerting about these echoes of a royal succession. This idealised and sentimentalised image of French rural society reflects a nostalgia for the archaic, and this nostalgia testifies to the supreme importance granted by Saint-Exupéry to notions of order, continuity and hierarchy. There is nothing here of peasant greed and suspicion, of rural ignorance and superstition, of family feuds over inheritance, of narrowness and stagnation, of female subjection to male. With blatant inconsistency, this recipe for a static society is recommended by a childless cosmopolitan who has left it all behind. In fact, this is not a description of the rural condition but an idyll, and this idyll is significant because it helps to define the central values of Saint-Exupéry's humanism. His preference for rurality implies a rejection of modern industrial society which reflects the paternalistic conservatism of the rural gentry among whom he was brought up in the south of France.

A series of reflections in *Terre des hommes* confirms the strength of these feelings. Near to death in the Libyan desert, Saint-Exupéry reaffirms his belief in the kind of life he has chosen: 'J'ai besoin de vivre. Dans les villes, il n'y a plus de vie humaine. Il ne s'agit point ici d'aviation. L'avion ce n'est pas une fin, c'est un moyen. Ce n'est pas pour l'avion que l'on risque sa vie. Ce n'est pas non plus pour sa charrue que le paysan laboure. Mais par l'avion, on quitte les villes et leurs comptables, et l'on retrouve une vérité paysanne' (*TH*, p. 149). It is hard not to feel that something of Saint-Exupéry's own early failures colours this condemnation, but there is a larger suspicion of urban life at work here, and a distaste for the urban masses that goes beyond condescension: 'Je ne comprends plus ces populations des trains de banlieue, ces hommes qui se croient des hommes, et qui cependant sont réduits, par une pression qu'ils ne sentent pas, comme les fourmis, à l'usage qui en est fait' (p. 150). Clearly Saint-Exupéry believes that industrialisation has denatured men,

severed them from '[le] langage des lignées paysannes', and
consigned them to an urban ghetto (p. 173).

This way of reducing the inhabitants of towns to a
uniform and undifferentiated mass strikes me as grossly
simplistic but in this, as in his implied reluctance to accept
that the industrial revolution cannot be disinvented, Saint-
Exupéry is something of a reactionary romantic. Certainly,
there is a degree of inconsistency in the way in which he tries
to separate commercial aviation from the commercial ends it
serves. In fact, the Latécoère Company belongs inescapably
to that world of 'accountants' which he affects to despise
elsewhere, and the skills, courage and dedication of the pilots
cannot be artificially disconnected from questions of profit
and loss. As a result, I do not feel that commercial aviation
can provide a satisfactory model of disinterested moral
action. Saint-Exupéry strains to prove otherwise. Here I have
in mind, especially, some of the entries which occur in the
notebooks he kept between 1935 and 1942.[7] Two entries in
the first notebook are particularly relevant. In the first, the
commitment to flying the mail is offered unequivocally as an
appropriate ideal to which to aspire in one's search for the
true vocation of man: 'La grandeur naît d'abord – et toujours – d'un but situé en dehors de soi (Aéropostale): dès que
l'on enferme l'homme en lui-même, il devient pauvre' (I,
p. 253). In the second, the writer shows himself to be more
uneasy about the moral status he is prepared to grant to
commercial aviation: 'Je n'admire point des hommes de
servir le courrier mais je tiens an mythe du courrier parce
qu'il forme de tels hommes' (I, p. 263).

Here the reference to 'le mythe du courrier' strikes me as
very significant, suggesting, as it does, that the important
thing for the pilot is not the airline's commercial goals but
the *mystique* of belonging, with one's comrades, to a new
chivalry of the air. In a word, Saint-Exupéry has to argue that
flying is not just a job but a calling, a way of serving an ideal.
As another chronicler of the life of action, Pierre Gascar, has
succinctly put it: 'il était nécessaire de substituer à l'avion le

---

[7] *Carnets*, ed. Pierre Chevrier (Paris, Gallimard, 1975).

sacerdoce qu'il rendait possible'.[8] In granting commercial flying this consecrated status, the airline becomes simply the medium through which the dedicated pilot finds a way of exploring the relationship of self to the world, and a means of establishing an acceptable moral order by forging bonds between human beings. In such a context, even the banal business of carrying letters between lovers or governments can be thought of as serving a larger purpose, as being engaged in a great humanist enterprise.

So the pilot serving the 'Line' is judged to be serving a purpose larger than himself, and the character of his service is defined in terms of the qualities associated with the shepherd, the peasant in his fields and the rural craftsman. That is to say, it is associated with humble and honest skills that protect, nurture and enhance life, and which create a community that is morally satisfying because it offers order, purpose and hierarchy – a proper place for everyone and everyone in his proper place. But this symbolic attempt to connect individual aspirations and the collective needs of society does not seem to me to be very convincingly made, though one can easily see how the individual can be satisfyingly related to his fellow professionals in the fraternity of flying.

Toward the end of *Terre des hommes,* and as a sequel to his account of his near-fatal ordeal in the Libyan desert, Saint-Exupéry poses a number of fundamental questions about the kind of man one should aspire to become and the conditions most likely to foster the nobility ('le seigneur') that lies dormant in all of us. He concludes by insisting that we must reject being part of the herd – 'Nous ne sommes pas un cheptel à l'engrais' (*TH,* p. 159), and, like the aviators who feature in the book, choose a testing vocation: 'le désert ou la ligne' (p. 159). The choice of vocation is important but so too are the occasions which can test it (p. 160). Two things need to be said about this passage: the nature of the spiritual life implied by its quasi-religious language is obscure, and it deals

---

[8] 'Quand l'homme d'action se fait écrivain', in R.-M. Albérès *et al., Saint-Exupéry* (Paris, Hachette, 1963), 124.

with individuals caught up in an exceptional discipline that
cannot easily be translated into the humdrum routines of
society. Can we all become heroes or saints? Subsequent
pages attempt to clarify precisely what it is that makes men
want to rise above habit, conditioning and inertia in order to
realise some finer self that is latent in them.

Here I propose to isolate a single incident that is used by
Saint-Exupéry to illustrate the idea of vocation, because it
crystallises the ambiguities of his position. It concerns the
Republican sergeant in the Spanish Civil War who is roused
from a deep sleep in order to go out on patrol: 'Le sergent fit
un dernier effort pour rentrer dans ses songes heureux, pour
refuser notre univers de dynamite, d'épuisement et de nuit
glacée; mais trop tard. Quelque chose s'imposait qui venait
du dehors' (*TH,* p. 164). This former book-keeper from
Barcelona is responding to a self-imposed duty, itself the
product of an obscure urge to fulfil himself by volunteering to
serve the Republican cause: 'tu éprouvais ici le sentiment de
t'accomplir, tu rejoignais l'universel; voici que toi, le paria, tu
étais reçu par l'amour' (p. 169). I confess to feeling a little
uneasy at the way in which a political choice here is being
surrounded with the language of mystical fervour, and my
unease is deepened by the long simile which Saint-Exupéry
employs in order to amplify his point. The sergeant's reaction
is likened to that of farmyard ducks which make spasmodic
efforts to fly, in answer to the call of the migratory wild ducks
passing overhead. The call rouses in them the instinct to fly,
to escape from the domesticated life of the farmyard and to
experience 'les étendues continentales, le goût des vents du
large, et la géographie des mers' (p. 166). This, in turn, sparks
off a simile involving the gazelles brought up in captivity at
Fort Juby which, at certain moments, press against the fence,
drawn irresistibly to the desert: 'Ce qu'elles cherchent vous le
savez, c'est l'étendue qui les accomplira. Elles veulent devenir gazelles et danser leur danse' (pp. 167-68).

Here I find a serious, and unacceptable, confusion between a free moral choice, on the one hand, and the great
instinctual drives of nature, on the other. What Saint-
Exupéry appears to say is that the only life worth living is

that which is put to the test, that in which man is permitted to realise his latent nature. Just as the gazelles need the desert and the taste of fear, so, it is argued, human beings need the challenge of an exacting vocation if they are to become fully themselves. Saint-Exupéry relates the sergeant's innate need for action and a transcendent cause to the rewards which finding such a cause provides – fraternal love and a sense of belonging. In this sense, Republicanism is the sergeant's 'calling', and in embracing its duties and discipline, he discovers union with others and a sense of meaning in his own life. For Saint-Exupéry, the actual motives which prompt the sergeant to join the Republicans are of little consequence when weighed against the benefits of belonging: 'Je me moque bien de connaître s'ils étaient sincères ou non, logiques ou non, les grands mots des politiciens qui t'ont peut-être ensemencé' (*TH*, p. 169). This is dangerous stuff. If the ideological content of our choices does not matter, how can we decide between the rival merits of entering a monastery or joining the S.S.? Certainly, common experience hardly suggests that we will unerringly choose the morally superior course of action.

This is a danger Saint-Exupéry briefly recognises a little later when he concedes how militarism and crude nationalism can pervert the human craving to serve and to belong (*TH*, pp. 174-75). Yet the sympathy and excitement which inform the vivid little scenes involving the Republican sergeant in Madrid, are surely revealing of the importance which Saint-Exupéry attaches to fraternity in his dream of an ideal moral order. The same is true of that incident in which Saint-Exupéry and his comrades are stranded in a part of the Sahara desert that is subject to raids from marauding tribesmen. They huddle behind a makeshift barrier of packing cases and discover a heightened sense of their common humanity and interdependence: 'Alors on s'épaule l'un à l'autre. On découvre que l'on appartient à la même communauté. On s'élargit par la découverte d'autres consciences' (*TH*, p. 37). At the moment when they are at their most vulnerable, they rediscover the riches of solidarity: 'nous avons bâti un village d'hommes' (p. 37). This moment in the hostile desert simply illustrates concretely one of Saint-Exupéry's earlier aphorisms: 'La grandeur d'un métier est peut-être, avant tout, d'unir des hommes: il n'est qu'un luxe véritable, et c'est celui des relations humaines' (p. 35).

It is obvious how much this conception of fraternity or solidarity, with its linked idea of community, relates to Saint-Exupéry's underlying preoccupation with the need for man to surpass himself, to go beyond narrow self-interest, and even beyond fear and weakness, in order to serve some larger common ideal. It is clear, too, how much all this owes to the particular and exceptional demands made on airmen engaged in blazing trails in commercial aviation. Of course, at one level, all modern means of communication imply a network of co-operation. The airline and its employees form a group united in interdependence and mutual aid. The radio-operators on the ground, the mechanics, flight controllers and office staff are as necessary to the pilots as the skills, dedication and courage of pilots and navigators are the necessary condition of their employment. The airline offers a network of communications, both internal and external, and, in *Terre des hommes,* this network is raised to the status of a metaphor of human fraternity and community. Men have common needs and aspirations, says Saint-Exupéry, though these may be lost sight of (as in the clashes between the aviators and the desert tribesmen). Only through open and sustained communication, through reciprocity, can human brotherhood be established. This sense of fraternity is shown as extending beyond the group of airline employees. It is also exemplified by the sergeant in temporary charge of the fort at Nouakchott and by the Bedouin who rescues Saint-Exupéry and Prévot when they are close to collapse.

But though fraternity comes from participating in a common enterprise characterised by interdependence and mutual aid, the bonds of fellowship, as portrayed in *Vol de nuit* and *Terre des hommes,* are fostered and secured by a framework of duty, discipline and obedience. The case of the sergeant from Barcelona illustrates this. Discipline and obedience imply leaders and led: strong leaders capable, when necessary, of imposing iron discipline; followers sufficiently convinced of the value of the common ideal they are serving, to accept the requirements of discipline and obedience. In *Vol de nuit* this creed finds its starkest expression in the figure of Rivière, the director of operations, though it is significant that the exaggerated cult of the will and discipline, which is embodied in him, is much attenuated in *Terre des hommes*. Even so, in the degree to which Rivière crystallises in his person the principles of paternalistic authority and respect for hierarchy, his spirit continues to live in the pages of *Terre des hommes*.

The central problem for us in assessing Rivière's creed can be put succinctly: what ends are served by the cult of will, discipline and obedience which he exemplifies? To begin with, it has to be said that, while Rivière can be tentative and obscure in the moral principles he expresses, he generally strikes us as being in confident possession of an austere doctrine of action. In articulating this doctrine, his language often comes close to the religious. Consequently, at the end of *Vol de nuit,* we are left with a strong impression that this voice, the one most frequently heard among the laconic pilots and their nearly silent women, is the voice of a mystic without a religion, or at least, without a supernatural religion. For Rivière, rules are like the rituals of religion: they may seem absurd to outsiders but they help to shape men. This task of moulding men is one he accepts with relish: 'L'homme était pour lui une cire vierge qu'il fallait pétrir. Il fallait donner une âme à cette matière, lui créer une volonté' (*VN,* p. 47). Later, when he is on the point of dismissing the old mechanic Roblet, Rivière repeats this view: 'Et les hommes sont de pauvres choses, et on les crée aussi' (p. 86). The language is instructive. Behind this impersonal 'on' is the God of the Old Testament, breathing life into clay and creating mankind. There is something frankly disconcerting, if not actually shocking, about the way in which Rivière arrogates these god-like powers to himself. At one point, he implicitly justifies these powers by his claim to be serving a higher cause: 'Ce n'est pas lui que j'ai congédié ainsi brutalement, c'est le mal dont il n'était pas responsable, peut-être, mais qui passait par lui' (p. 86).

But can evil be convincingly equated with a momentary lapse in the working practices of a mechanic? If Rivière smuggles this metaphysical concept into the world of practical work, it is because he has to cast around in order to find some ultimate, transcendent principle to which he can appeal and which will justify the harshness of the regime he imposes on air-crew and ground-staff alike. Error must be punished, men like Roblet must, if necessary, be humiliated, even though Rivière is quite uncertain of the precise nature of the values he is invoking: 'Je ne sais pas l'exacte valeur de la vie humaine, ni de la justice, ni du chagrin. Je ne sais pas exactement ce que vaut la joie d'un homme. Ni une main qui tremble. Ni la pitié, ni la douceur...' (*VN*, p. 89). One is tempted to say that a man who is so remote from common human experience is a bit of a monster. In any event, the rigour he displays goes beyond the individual concerned. It aims to create a lasting achievement that will testify to the creative human spirit: 'Mais durer, mais créer, échanger son corps périssable...' (p. 89). And this lasting monument is held to represent a kind of immortality, not for the individual but for the community, the civilisation of which he is part. Which is why Rivière approves of the Inca ruler who is prepared to sacrifice his subjects so that he can bequeath a sun temple to posterity: 'Au nom de quelle dureté, ou de quel étrange amour, le conducteur de peuples d'autrefois, contraignant ses foules à tirer ce temple sur la montagne, leur imposa-t-il donc de dresser leur éternité?' (p. 131).

To use the word 'love' in this context is to grant a blood-stained superstition a dignity I cannot feel it deserves. Surely, the value of the Inca ruler's achievement depends on whether it is brought about by tyranny and coercion. A medieval cathedral erected with the free participation of the faithful is one thing, an Inca temple built on slavery, quite another. There is great confusion of values here, and disturbing undertones of authoritarianism. One looks in vain for an adequate and compelling definition of the values which might justify so rigorous a discipline and so complete an obedience. As Rivière himself puts it: 'nous agissons toujours comme si quelque chose dépassait, en valeur, la vie humaine... Mais quoi?' (p. 130). It is reasonable to question whether individual human happiness is a sufficient moral goal, but this does not dispose of the need to find convincing alternatives.

In the final analysis, I cannot feel that the airline and its exploits in *Vol de nuit* are simply symbolic of a more general human aspiration to create an enduring monument that will fully engage individuals and inspire them to rise above their normal limits. The fact is that *Vol de nuit* renders the activity of flying in altogether too concrete and specific a way, one too much rooted in the economics of a regular mail service, to be thought of as purely figurative. All Rivière's moral prescriptions have to be seen as arising from, and applying to, the activity of commercial aviation at a particular stage in its development. As a consequence, when Rivière asks if there is 'un devoir plus grand que celui d'aimer' (p. 131), his own creed does not seem to me to supply it. In this creed, men are never important in themselves but only for what they accomplish, and so there is something dangerously totalitarian about the demands he makes on them and about the indifference he displays toward the ordinary norms of justice. One can readily admire the courage and dedication of the pilots but this cult of the mail-service is spurious because it represents a deification of the will and of energy irrespective of the ends to which they are applied. Hence the moral scheme of *Vol de nuit,* as epitomised in Rivière, is fatally flawed.

**4**

# Man and Woman

B Y drawing exclusively on his personal experience of commercial aviation in North Africa and South America, Saint-Exupéry necessarily conjures up the world of pioneer airmen as if it were a uniquely male preserve. But immediately one looks beyond the development of commercial airlines proper, the era of pioneering flying in the 1920s and 1930s can be seen to be greatly indebted to the achievements of outstanding female aviators like Amelia Earhart, Amy Mollison and Jean Batty. Not even in the more discursive pages of *Terre des hommes,* where there is a tendency to dwell on epochmaking moments in the history of modern aviation, is there any allusion to the presence of women in the air. By restricting himself to the exploits of the 'Line', and to the ordeals of Guillaumet, Mermoz and himself, Saint-Exupéry can be free to articulate his preferred, and highly traditional, picture of the relations between the sexes.

Not that *Vol de nuit* and *Terre des hommes* display much in the way of formal characterisation. Essentially, what we encounter in both texts is the subordination of individuals to types. Characters tend to be emblematic of certain well-defined qualities operating within a fixed moral scheme. There is limited curiosity about the concrete circumstances of individual lives, little sense of the complexity of human motives, and not much mystery or surprise attaching to the persons involved in the narratives. In *Vol de nuit* and *Terre des hommes,* Saint-Exupéry's preference is for producing 'voices' rather than fully developed characters; that is, convenient embodiments of certain attitudes to life rather than specific individuals who are sufficiently explored to make them interesting as autonomous beings. Hence, as I have suggested in chapter 1, the use of names (Fabien/Pellerin/ Rivière) that point to styles of life rather than to singular individuals.

Principally what we have is a highly stylised dichotomy between 'virile' and 'feminine' voices, and this dichotomy tends to rest on a very traditional view of the nature of the sexes, in which men are active and dominating agents and women are passive sufferers. Indeed, it is not too much to say of Saint-Exupéry's men and women, as they emerge from these texts, that they represent two distinct orders of being, two imperatives that are in conflict. It could, of course, be argued that the male/female dichotomy in Saint-Exupéry's narratives represents, in schematic fashion, divisions that exist within the author's own personality, each facet of his nature being given imaginative representation in the male/ female characters he has created (more particularly in *Vol de nuit*). However, I personally feel that the female characters are much too lightly and conventionally explored to make this argument convincing.

Obviously I would not want to say that there is a complete absence of individualising psychological and physical detail, especially in *Vol de nuit*. It is true that, in this text, Fabien is little explored, though we do learn a certain amount about him from his inner monologues and his reactions to the crises which confront him. In addition, inspector Robineau supplies us with a few details about his private life: his ready laughter, for example, or the fact that he has only been married for six weeks. Even so, he emerges more as an heroic silhouette than a developed character. He is interesting less for what we glean about him than for the virtues which he embodies. Certainly, Fabien's wife has more detail lavished on her but here too, as I hope to show shortly, this reveals less about her than it does about Rivière's way of looking at women. In a similar fashion, we learn of Pellerin's modesty and professionalism from the reticent and technical report he gives to Rivière about the cyclone he has had to contend with (*VN*, pp. 42-43), but we learn nothing else. As for the pilot preparing for the European run (to whom I shall return when discussing Saint-Exupéry's depiction of women characters), he is ren-

dered wholly from the outside, in terms of the virile attributes
which the author tends to grant to all pilots. In much the
same way, the pilot on the Paraguay run is sketched in
summarily, in a style that comes perilously close to a carica-
ture of the laconic manliness that is common in the novels of
Hemingway. These exchanges from *Vol de nuit* convey the
flavour very well: 'C'est toi qui continues?... La Patagonie est
là?... Il fait très beau. Fabien a disparu?' (*VN*, p. 182).

Even in the less 'invented' pages of *Terre des hommes,*
Guillaumet and Mermoz tend to be represented with a
minimum of concrete personal detail that might suggest that
they have a life outside their aircraft. They are simply
presented as models of manly courage and professional dedication, as emblems rather than persons. This tendency to
move beyond individuals in order to represent the ideal
virtues which they embody is graphically reinforced in both
texts, though particularly in *Vol de nuit,* by the imagery with
which Saint-Exupéry surrounds his airmen. Whether in the
actual autobiographical material of *Terre des hommes* or the
thinly fictionalised autobiography of *Vol de nuit,* the world of
the pilots is consistently portrayed as an epic realm in which
heroic males struggle with the elements and surpass themselves in the process. Earlier on in this study, I isolated what
appeared to me to be a deeply significant fondness, on
Saint-Exupéry's part, for associating fliers with the virtues
and simplicities of a timeless, rustic world. In this context,
they are seen as exemplifying the nurturing and creative
impulses in human beings and as belonging to a stable moral
order in which respect for authority and a certain hierarchy
in human relations is matched by a readiness to accept
discipline and obedience as a way of guaranteeing the survival of that moral order. This basically modest picture of them
as servants of a larger moral purpose is, however, frequently
displaced by a far more potent imagery suggestive of a new
order of chivalry but also of the disdainful superiority of a
new élite.

The pilot is most commonly envisaged as the natural
leader of men and is given a range of attributes: warrior or
knight-errant, consecrated priest, or god-like bringer of life.

There is an admixture of more modest images of the airman but, not infrequently, even these merge with more prestigious allusions. Take the case of Guillaumet's ordeal in the Andes, as given in *Terre des hommes*. Initially, the flier is given heroic status, but he also comes over strongly as a repository of human wisdom and model of responsible leadership. Later, however, when Saint-Exupéry is lost in the Libyan desert, he conjures up Guillaumet's example in the Andes and, immediately, the veteran pilot becomes the focus of almost superstitious awe and is viewed as a powerful talisman capable of warding off death. Elsewhere in the same text, the portrait of the young pilot as nothing more than the modest 'guardian' of the mail is quickly superseded when his own idealistic mission is contrasted with the lives of 'les passants ignorants' and 'ces barbares' (*TH,* p. 16) among whom he moves in disdainful anonymity, like a disguised prince muffled up in his overcoat.

Such moments in the narrative, when humbler images of the airman appear, are scattered and weak if compared with others in which he is surrounded with an aura of glamour. In the early pages of *Vol de nuit,* Fabien is initially depicted as a weary conqueror poised over his imperial domains: 'Il était semblable à un conquerant, au soir de ses conquêtes, qui se penche sur les terres de l'empire, et découvre l'humble bonheur des hommes' (*VN,* p. 19). Later his flight is described as a military campaign: 'marches, contremarches, territoires gagnés qu'il faut rendre' (p. 69). This image of the aviator as warrior-king is prolonged in the curiously feudal disdain expressed by Pellerin when he looks down from his cockpit on the ground-staff: 'Il tenait ce peuple dans ses larges mains, comme des sujets, puisqu'il pouvait les toucher, les entendre et les insulter' (p. 34). When, in the final chapter, the mail-plane for Europe takes off, the young pilot is described as laughing for joy and his teeth are compared with those of a wild beast ('un jeune fauve'), an image of the savage hunter which is reinforced by Rivière's own allusion to him as passing overhead like 'le pas formidable d'une armée en marche dans les étoiles' (p. 187). This entire cluster of images associates the airmen with war, old-style conquest and victorious warriors. Such images reinforce the cult of will which is pervasive in this text and the prestige of the pilot as man of ruthless action, before whom (in Rivière's phrase) cities fall (p. 65).

Elsewhere, however, Saint-Exupéry seems anxious to counter whatever in these images might be construed as mere appetite for dangerous living, irrespective of the ends being served. That is why, in *Terre des hommes,* he insists that the heroic Guillaumet is no crude adventurer and is not to be confused with 'les toréadors et les joueurs' (p. 48). This need to dignify the profession of flying and to persuade us that it is a noble calling – is not Guillaumet associated with 'la noblesse du montagnard'? (p. 49) – finds its most sustained expression in two clusters of images. In the first, the aviator is associated with legend and knights-errant; in the second, with the religious calling.

The world of the flier is frequently depicted by Saint-Exupéry as a legendary world or, as he puts it in the early pages of *Terre des hommes,* 'un monde fabuleux, plein de pièges, de trappes, de falaises brusquement surgies, et de remous qui eussent déraciné des cèdres' (*TH,* p. 11). This image of the skies as a fairy-tale world, full of wonders and surprises, is prolonged in a subsequent passage: 'Des dragons noirs défendaient l'entrée des vallées, des gerbes d'éclairs couronnaient les crêtes' (pp. 11-12). This in turn is developed through an allusion to the veteran flier, Bury, an archetype of the strong, silent man: 'il laissait, sous sa rude écorce, percer l'ange qui avait vaincu le dragon' (p. 12). The same figure persists a little later (p. 21) when Saint-Exupéry writes of 'les dragons noirs et les crêtes couronnées d'une chevelure d'éclairs bleus'. The significance of this series of images is clear: the airman is a story-book hero, a slayer of dragons, like Saint George, and by extension, a member of a new order of chivalry. A variant of these images, which Saint-Exupéry deploys on other pages of *Terre des hommes,* supports this general sense of flying as a fairy-tale kingdom over which the chivalrous pilot is poised: 'Et peu à peu, l'Espagne de ma carte devenait, sous la lampe, un pays de contes de fées' (p. 16). Nothing could illustrate more vividly Saint-Exupéry's desire to grant flying a status beyond that of an ordinary job and to surround it with a special aura of mystery, nobility and service.

This set of associations is amplified in the second cluster of images to which I have referred, that of the religious vocation. At this point, it is worth emphasising that these allusions to a spiritual domain are very general in character and do not depend on any clearly articulated system of beliefs. When, in *Terre des hommes,* Saint-Exupéry gives an account of waking on the morning of his first mail run, he writes of it as a grave and solemn occasion, 'le jour de la consécration' (*TH,* p. 17), with overtones of entering an order of priesthood. Later he will speak of himself as submitting to the 'rites sacrés du métier' (p. 20) and of receiving his 'baptism' in the skies (p. 21), a baptism that signals entry into a way of life that is superior to the dull and trivial routines of the ground staff. He literally and figuratively rises above them, gives up the commonplace pleasures of the world – typified by the shops full of sparkling Christmas gifts – and feels elation at doing so: 'et je goûtais l'ivresse orgueilleuse du renoncement' (p. 17). At a later stage in his career, when he is stranded in the desert, Saint-Exupéry reverts to this imagery and likens the stranded men to members of an austere religious order: 'Un style dur pour trappistes' (p. 37).

The cumulative effect of these images is to project flying for the airline as an almost esoteric calling, confined to initiates who sacrifice themselves to a higher service. The spiritual thrust of such imagery is taken to its limit when the aviator is identified either as the bearer of life – a seed blown by the wind on to sterile places (p. 61) – or as the very principle of life against death. Such is the case with Guillaumet – 'quand il luttait au nom de sa Création, contre la mort' (p. 48). In all these ways, Saint-Exupéry conscripts language so as to confer a high dignity on the profession he has chosen to follow, to persuade us that the quality of this élite is superior to that of common men, and to coax us into accepting that obedience, discipline and self-discipline are the necessary conditions of this excellence. Yet this ethic of service and renunciation has its ugly side in a sort of contemptuous condescension toward ordinary people, most of whom, like the mechanic Leroux in *Vol de nuit,* have their entire lives consumed by drudgery. There is something truly chilling about Rivière's comment: 'Les petits bourgeois des petites villes tournent le soir autour de leur kiosque à musique et Rivière pensait: "Juste ou injuste envers eux, cela n'a pas de sens: ils n'existent pas".' (*VN,* pp. 46-47). The same vast condescension is echoed in the author/narrator of *Terre des hommes* when he berates the unfortunate citizen of Toulouse: 'tu es un petit bourgeois de Toulouse. Nul ne t'a saisi par les épaules quand il était temps encore. Maintenant, la glaise dont tu es formé a séché, et s'est durcie, et nul en toi ne saurait désormais réveiller le musicien endormi ou le poète, ou l'astronome qui peut-être t'habitait d'abord' (*TH,* p. 21). Here the definition of worth is too exclusively identified with artistic or scientific creativity, values scarcely applicable to the rustic models which Saint-Exupéry is so fond of invoking elsewhere.

To judge from the exalted images of airline pilots with which Saint-Exupéry presents us, the process of characterising males in *Vol de nuit* and *Terre des hommes* constantly eludes psychological or social realism in favour of idealised types, and this is a necessary consequence of the kind of moral vision which informs these texts. But it might be objected that Rivière and Robineau do not, in practice, conform to these limited types. Indeed, I would want to argue that, to a certain degree, they are both individualised, filled out, and made interesting according to more traditional modes of characterisation. Here I am not concerned, as I was in chapter 3, to look at the intrinsic merits of Rivière's creed of leadership, but only at his status as a character. If the fate of Fabien helps to unify the narrative of *Vol de nuit,* it is Rivière who dominates it, though whether as developed character or as characterful vehicle for a set of moral ideas, is another matter.

The first thing that needs to be said is that Rivière's moral ideas are not only densely present at all those moments when he is speaking directly in his own person, but are also reinforced by the third-person commentary of the narrator, as when he insists: 'Il était indifférent à Rivière de paraître juste ou injuste' (*VN, p. 46*). The result is to make him seem so flawlessly self-consistent, so monolithic, that it is usually difficult to believe that he is other than a mere mouthpiece. The same ideas recur and are driven home. To this extent, it is natural that Rivière should tend to emerge as the stereotype, and perhaps admired model, of an authoritarian leader. But there are clues which point to other dimensions in Rivière's fictive personality and, though these are slight and fragmentary, they are enough to persuade us that he has a life and possibilities beyond the moral precepts he enunciates. In a word, there are enough concrete particulars present to rescue him from being nothing but an emblem.

This 'éternel voyageur' moving restlessly about the airline offices and caught up in perpetual anxious concern for his pilots, is not just the model of a paternalist. The vigils at night and the long years of responsibility have taken their toll of him, inducing a profound weariness that is brought home to us in a few telling human details. He is conscious of ageing and mortality: '"Je vieillis... Tout cela est donc si proche?..."' (*VN*, p. 29). He is prey to a fit of melancholy which prompts him to ask the workman Leroux a surprising question that helps to individuate him: 'Vous vous êtes beaucoup occupé d'amour, Leroux, dans votre vie?' (p. 30). In Leroux's wry and dismissive response, Rivière recognises sadly the emotional impoverishment of his own life and the fact that there is nothing he can now do to alter it. When, later, he rejoices to note how Leroux's ugliness has been the cause of the latter's total dedication to his job – '"Regardez-moi ça comme c'est beau, cette laideur qui repousse l'amour..."' (p. 62) – this brutal, left-handed compliment offsets the sympathy of the original enquiry and confirms that we are dealing with a complicated man.

Certainly, Rivière's injuction – 'Aimez ceux que vous commandez. Mais sans le leur dire' (p. 64) – like his sense of being above the common rut of mortals ('les médiocres'), or the stoicism contained in his boast: 'Pour se faire aimer, il suffit de plaindre. Je ne plains guère ou je le cache' (p. 103), is consistent with the creed of a hard leader. But these

qualities are shown to coexist with physical vulnerability and
with strains of doubt and tenderness. A nagging and debilitat-
ing pain in his side temporarily immobilises him, leaving him
(in an image of pathos) 'ligoté comme un vieux lion' (p. 83);
the fatigue it induces provokes doubts about his entire style of
leadership: 'Il lui vint une certaine lassitude d'avoir tracé si
durement cette route. Il pensa que la pitié est bonne' (p. 84).
And even the harsh creed of survival implied in Rivière's
formula – 'Ce qui est vivant bouscule tout pour vivre et crée,
pour vivre, ses propres lois' (p. 105) – is offset by other
moments in the text when a quite different sensibility is at
work. I think of the way in which Rivière responds to the
beauties of the night – 'une vaste nef' (p. 58), and of the
reticent but deep sympathy he feels for Simone Fabien when
she comes for news to the airline offices (p. 162). I think,
above all, of the moving fashion in which he is shown as
identifying with Fabien's last hours. All this suggests a more
explored and complex picture of Rivière than that conjured
up by the term 'martinet', but I still feel that the way in
which Rivière is left to spell out his gospel of discipline and
leadership does create a sort of barrier which regularly dis-
rupts the fictional flow of *Vol de nuit.*

Paradoxically, the character of Robineau, who tends to be
portrayed as a pathetic nonentity, is fleshed out with a good
deal of detail and conveys a stronger sense of life (even if it is
a damaged life) than either Rivière or the minor characters in
the narrative: the airmen, the mechanics Leroux and Roblet,

Simone Fabien, and the wife of the pilot on the European
run. In fact, I think he is a genuinely comic creation, a rare
phenomenon in Saint-Exupéry's writing, who manages to
elude being destroyed by the contempt of Rivière and the
narrator. In the car which brings Pellerin from the airfield to
Buenos Aires, Robineau is still just a shadowy 'inspecteur
morne' (*VN*, p. 34) who does not say a word during the ride,
though we are given access to his thoughts and recollections.
At this juncture, the narrator singles out Robineau's Adam's
apple and this highlighting of a mildly absurd physical
feature prepares us for the generally mocking treatment he
will receive in the text.

He is described as carrying his melancholy air around with him like a piece of luggage and as being cut off from his colleagues by his clumsiness and self-importance: 'il était empêtré de ses grandes mains et de sa dignité d'inspecteur' (p. 44). He is a buttoned-up little man, quite unable to join in the easy intimacy of the company mess, set apart from the operational direction of the airline, and barely tolerated by those more actively involved. As the narrator wittily and woundingly puts it: 'Il n'était guère aimé, car un inspecteur n'est pas créé pour les délices de l'amour' (p. 44). Rivière puts him down at every turn: 'L'inspecteur Robineau est prié de nous fournir, non des poèmes, mais des rapports' (p. 44). As a result of never being consulted on matters of importance, he comes down heavily on minor infringements of regulations. He is thought by Rivière to have his uses but not to be very bright, and by insisting on the letter of the law, he becomes a figure of fun and an object of keen dislike by the airline staff. His inflexibility is summed up in a hilarious fashion. All pilots benefit from a no-crash bonus but if they are forced down, even if through no fault of their own, and damage their aircraft, they are still punished. Robineau's verdict is a parody of bureaucracy: 'je regrette même infiniment, mais il fallait avoir la panne ailleurs' (p. 46).

Petty and unimaginative in his application of the rules, obsessed with administrative detail, Robineau is also starved of friendship and leads a drab private life in an anonymous hotel room. The tone in which all these facts are related to us is notably unsympathetic and generates a kind of unforgiving comedy at Robineau's expense. We are invited to note 'le corps infligé d'un gênant eczéma' (p. 53), so as to prompt us to add this unsavoury detail to his prominent Adam's apple and clumsy hands. We are also asked to deplore his shocking taste in shirts and his scrawny mistress whose photograph adorns his walls. As a result, we are forced to share Pellerin's reaction to Robineau: 'Alignant dans un ordre misérable ses trésors, il étalait devant le pilote sa misère. Un eczéma moral. Il montrait sa prison' (p. 60). And to divert us from the brutal distaste displayed here, the narrator quickly moves us forward with a further comic touch in which the pathetic Robineau produces a handful of black pebbles and confesses that geology is his real 'passion' (p. 60).

All these disparaging details are assembled so as to contrast the hollow bureaucrat with the man of action (Pellerin) and the inspiring leader (Rivière). It is a comic technique, and it works. In the process, however, it reveals to us a more complicated and interesting figure than the near-stereotypes who surround him, and the level of our interest is raised in the final chapters that focus on the loss of Fabien. Here, though Robineau has so small a part to play – 'Ce garçon médiocre, maintenant inutile, n'avait plus de sens' (p. 163) – he gives evidence, notably in chapter XXI, of much good will and of renewed respect and understanding for the pain and loneliness that are inseparable from Rivière's exercise of authority. Whatever our final judgement on him, we are, at least, allowed to uncover in Robineau a truer sense of the complexity of human experience.

What maintains our interest in Robineau is the impression of human idiosyncrasy which he conveys. What strikes us about the female characters of *Vol de nuit* is the degree to which they conform to sexual stereotypes. They hardly figure at all in *Terre des hommes*: shadowy forms in the interstices of the action, except for the two fey little girls who charm Saint-Exupéry in the dilapidated mansion near Concordia. Even in *Vol de nuit,* only two female characters have any degree of detail lavished on them: Simone Fabien and the young wife of the pilot about to set out for Europe. Elsewhere in the text, women exist in a ghostly way on the periphery of male lives: they have no place at all in the life of Leroux; Roblet's wife is simply a blurred figure in a family group; and Robineau's mistress is just an emblem of the impoverishment of his emotional life, not a proof of the power of women.

Of the main female characters, it can be said that they conform neatly to the classic dichotomy expressed by the nineteenth-century English writer, Charles Kingsley: 'For men must work, and women must weep'. For example, we are given quite a long scene between the pilot on the European run and his wife, but throughout it, she is simply the mirror to him. It is significant that we learn nothing concrete about her physical appearance – colour of eyes or hair, for example. The narrative point of view is such that we are not allowed to dwell on her body and charms, but only on a kind of worshipful image of her husband as seen through her adoring eyes: 'Elle admirait cette poitrine nue, bien carénée, elle pensait à un beau navire' (*VN,* p. 93), or: 'Elle regardait ces bras solides' (p. 94), or again: 'Ces larges épaules pesaient déjà contre le ciel' (p. 96). These flattering images of the male as Adonis are further enhanced when more potent attributes than physical strength and beauty are grafted on to them. The pilot's wife associates his carrying of the mail with a great enterprise, like that involving the fate of a city ('comme du sort d'une ville'), and she thinks of him as a 'jeune dieu' singled out for a life of sacrifice (p. 94). She sees him also as a free agent, unlike her tethered self, bent on the 'conquest' of plains, towns and mountains (p. 95), and when he puts on his flying gear, she notes: 'Il s'habillait. Pour cette fête, il choisissait les étoffes les plus rudes, les cuirs les plus lourds, il s'habillait comme un paysan. Plus il devenait lourd, plus elle l'admirait. Elle-même bouclait cette ceinture, tirait ces bottes' (pp. 96-97). In this quasi-feudal ceremony, she is the subservient squire to his lordly knight, to this warrior donning his armour before he leaves for the wars.

In the shadow of this dominant male, who, significantly, picks her up effortlessly as if she were a child, the wife is defined as one who serves and ministers. Specifically, she smoothes the sheet on his bed: 'elle effaçait du doigt ce pli, cette ombre, cette houle, elle apaisait ce lit, comme, d'un doigt divin, la mer' (p. 93). In this image of maternal solicitude, borrowed from Saint-Exupéry's childhood memories, the wife is established as protectress, powerful enough to ward off danger. The 'divine' touch of the mother is transferred to her in a setting slightly coloured with erotic detail. These feelings of comfort and protection are revived when the wife is described as feeding and keeping watch over her husband: 'Elle l'avait nourri, veillé et caressé' (p. 94). Such images reinforce a profoundly traditional and male-centred view of relations between men and women, and render woman as

*Freudian*

either nurse/mother or child/wife for whom the superior husband is always an enigma and whose male world of action she can never enter. This worship of the mysterious and unpredictable male by the adoring and subservient female possesses a distinctly archaic quality which is intensified by the allusions to knightly prowess. As an image of the relations between men and women, it has, I think, to be read as a reflection of the narrator's nostalgia for social forms and traditions which were already anachronistic at the time his novel appeared.

Nor is this picture appreciably modified in the case of Fabien's wife, Simone, who is seen principally through Rivière's eyes. His replies to her queries about the overdue Fabien are revealing of the sexual stereotyping which takes place in this novel. Simone, whose voice is described by Rivière as 'petite voix lointaine, tremblante' (p. 128), is viewed by him not so much as an individual woman but as the female principle of nurture and solicitude at odds with the male values of action and decision. Her feminine world is defined in blatantly conventional terms as: 'Celui d'une clarté de lampe sur la table du soir, d'une chair qui réclamait sa chair, d'une patrie d'espoirs, de tendresses, de souvenirs' (p. 129). This is the woman of old-fashioned women's magazines. When, at the end of their telephone conversation, Simone lapses into silence, Rivière concludes: 'Elle n'écoutait plus. Elle était retombée, presque à ses pieds, *lui semblait-il,* ayant usé ses faibles poings contre le mur' (p. 129, my italics). Of course, this is completely conjectural on Rivière's part but it speaks eloquently of his settled view that it is in the nature of women to be frail and to collapse at the feet of men when they are faced with cruel realities.

A little later, convinced that Fabien is now lost, Rivière reflects: 'Rivière connaît la femme de Fabien inquiète et tendre: cet amour à peine lui fut prêté, comme un jouet à un enfant pauvre' (p. 154). Here the oblique tribute to Simone's feminine qualities and regret for the premature ending of her marriage, is balanced by the condescension implicit in his last phrase where Simone is relegated to the status of a child being given a toy by an adult male. When Simone finally arrives at the airline offices, the picture which the narrator gives of her amplifies the traits that have been singled out so far. In this world of urgent male work, she evokes images of pure domesticity: 'le lit entrouvert, le café servi, un bouquet de fleurs...' (p. 160). She is also represented as an intruder, 'une vérité ennemie', and is associated by the staff with 'le monde sacré du bonheur' (p. 161). While feeling genuine pity for her plight, Rivière too identifies her with the domestic round: 'ses fleurs, son café servi, sa chair jeune'. After a short while, she drifts away, wearing 'un sourire presque humble' (p. 162), doubtless because she is in awe of this male world where she has no rightful place. One final image of Simone surfaces in Rivière's mind: 'Rivière pense à la main de Fabien, qui tient pour quelques minutes encore sa destinée dans les commandes. Cette main qui a caressé. Cette main qui s'est posée sur une poitrine et y a levé le tumulte, comme une main divine. Cette main qui s'est posée sur un visage, et qui a changé ce visage. Cette main qui était miraculeuse' (p. 154). Here, most revealingly, Simone is the absent, faceless and unnamed object of these attentions in which a godlike male confers the privilege of his love on a passive female who receives it as a miraculous gift. All this is far less brutal than the flagrantly sexist fiction of Saint-Exupéry's contemporaries, Montherlant and Drieu la Rochelle, though it may be unconsciously funnier than either. At the very least, it presents the reader of today with a profoundly arrested and unsatisfactory picture of the relations between the sexes, a picture marked by a striking absence of reciprocity.

But if the sexual stereotyping of *Vol de nuit* confronts today's reader with serious difficulties, it also impoverishes the imaginative scope of the text, robbing the principal female characters of substance. In their dependence and immaturity, they are more like girls than women. Nor is this picture significantly altered by the discreet erotic detail which the narrator introduces from time to time. Such women are simply convenient embodiments of idealised femininity and, as has been perceptively said of them, they are not taken from adult experience but from the world of childhood (*8*, p. 197). The child-women of *Vol de nuit* reflect the sentimental nostalgia we meet later, in the pages of *Terre des hommes*, where the author/narrator recalls 'ces deux fées', the two fanciful little girls in the old house at Concordia, who enchant him with their naivety and playfulness, and whose loss of sexual innocence in marriage he implicitly laments: 'Et l'imbécile emmène la princesse en esclavage' (*TH*, p. 74).

The source of Saint-Exupéry's inability to portray women adequately in the fiction of *Vol de nuit* or, it might be added, in his first novel *Courrier sud*, lies in his own childhood and, more particularly, in the intensity of his emotional attachment to his mother. His surviving letters are eloquent testimony to this, as a few examples will serve to illustrate. A letter written to his mother in 1922 (when he was twenty-two) includes such phrases as: 'On se sentait en sécurité dans votre maison, on était en sécurité dans votre maison, on n'était rien qu'à vous, c'était bon... En bien, maintenant c'est la même chose, c'est vous qui êtes le refuge, c'est vous qui savez tout, qui faites tout oublier et qu'on le veuille ou non, on se sent un tout petit garçon!' (*Lettres*, p. 78). A year later, October 1923, he writes: 'J'abdique entre vos mains, c'est vous qui parlerez aux puissances supérieures et tout ira. Je suis comme un tout petit gosse maintenant, je me réfugie près de vous...' (*Lettres*, p. 80). Finally, in a letter written from Cairo on 3 January 1936, after his rescue from the Libyan desert, Saint-Exupéry confesses: 'J'ai pleuré en lisant votre petit mot si plein de sens, parce que je vous ai appelé dans le désert. J'avais pris de grandes colères contre le départ de tous les hommes, contre ce silence, et j'appelais ma maman' (*Lettres*, pp. 144-45).

The powerful bonds uniting mother and son could hardly be more vividly illustrated than in this poignant confession of a thirty-five-year-old man who, near to death, turns in imagination not to his beautiful, if wilful and tempestuous, wife but to his mother. Here, it seems to me, is a vital clue to Saint-Exupéry's failure to create satisfactory women characters in *Vol de nuit*. In identifying male love so completely with the mother, the writer cannot find an appropriate way of locating sexuality in his fictional wives. They have to be reduced either to ministering angels or else to child-women, quite lacking in independence and barely touched by adult passion. The result is to impoverish the art of characterisation.

# 5

# Style and Vision

'A treatise on leadership written in the form of a novel in the language of a poet.' This comment on *Vol de nuit* by one of Saint-Exupéry's main biographers (*1*, p. 230) wittily epitomises the way in which his writings elude conventional literary genres. Does *Vol de nuit* display the design of a novel or is it a thinly veiled form of self-disclosure? And is *Terre des hommes* an assemblage of occasional journalistic pieces artfully rearranged or a long meditation on the meaning of human life that happens to use disparate materials as illustrations? The problem of genre does not seem to me to be crucial here. It is far more important for our understanding of Saint-Exupéry that we should be attentive to the precise ways in which the vision and sensibility that inform *Vol de nuit* and *Terre des hommes* are translated through specific stylistic devices and recurring clusters of images.

First, it has to be said that, in spite of Saint-Exupéry's own doubts about the adequacy of language to convey the variety and richness of lived experience, we are dealing with two texts that are never remotely flat or naturalistic. On the contrary, Saint-Exupéry's language is often highly charged, densely imaged and lyrical in tone. It alternates between brevity, ellipsis and concentration, on the one hand, and elaboration, repetition and expansiveness, on the other (*7*, p. 46). The first set of characteristics dominates in *Vol de nuit*, the second in *Terre des hommes*. Within the framework of these dominant stylistic tendencies, I want to examine the vehicles which Saint-Exupéry finds appropriate to convey both the picture which he projects of man in his physical relations with the earth, and the moral and spiritual vision that he also tries to express. In the first case, we need to recall the airman's awakening to the earth as an ageless and stony place which is also man's natural habitat and a challenge to him to create a specifically human order. The second case is linked to the belief that man is impelled to aspire to an ideal self, an aspiration that releases his creative energies and involves him in the pursuit of a moral and spiritual order which transcends him as an individual and is defined in terms of interdependence, fraternity and community.

In trying to connect Saint-Exupéry's 'vision' of the world with specific features of his style in *Vol de nuit* and *Terre des hommes,* I want to begin with his use of simile, a figure he exploits more often than metaphor though, as we shall see, several of his favourite images are metaphoric in character. In the first of his notebooks, Saint-Exupéry offers a definition of the process of analogy in literature: 'L'image analogique se fonde sur sa faculté à former synthèse, à réunir les diverses parties d'un tout' (I, p. 298). Now, this process of bringing together seemingly disparate things in a single unified image or synthesis appears more properly to be a definition of how metaphor works. Simile rests on a simpler function, that of comparing two things of different kinds, and, in practice, this is the figure which Saint-Exupéry prefers. His preference is revealing of a certain stylistic timidity, of a tendency to spell out rather fully the relations between the real and the imaginary.

A number of Saint-Exupéry's similes are long, and some are overextended. I have referred elsewhere to the very lengthy simile, occupying some two pages of *Terre des hommes* (pp. 166-68), in which man's aspiration to reach a higher self is likened to the way in which farmyard ducks respond to the call of the migrant wild ducks passing overhead ('L'appel sauvage a réveillé en eux je ne sais quel vestige sauvage'), or the manner in which tame gazelles are drawn irresistibly to the desert ('Elles veulent devenir gazelles, et danser leur danse'). I have already argued that this simile seeks, very inappropriately, to identify human free will and choice with the great instinctual drives. I am tempted to add that the over-extension of the simile reflects Saint-Exupéry's uncertainty about its validity, though the use of the 'natural' as a model for human ethics is rooted in the highly traditional world-picture to which Saint-Exupéry habitually appeals.

In fact, a number of Saint-Exupéry's extended similes are revealing of his preference for traditional forms and values. As an example, I would recall a moment in *Terre des hommes* where the pilot is made aware of the importance of the plane as an instrument for rediscovering the familiar world. His situation is translated into a simile: 'Semblable au paysan qui fait sa tournée dans son domaine et qui prévoit, à mille signes, la marche du printemps, la menace du gel, l'annonce de la pluie, le pilote de métier, lui aussi, déchiffre des signes de neige, des signes de brume, des signes de nuit bienheureuse' (*TH,* p. 30). I have already indicated how the identification of pilot and peasant fits in with Saint-Exupéry's underlying social philosophy, but, in this stylistic context, I would also wish to stress that the accumulation of details about the weather within this simile reinforces simply but effectively the congruence between these two lives. This sense of congruity is not always so clear.

Elsewhere in *Terre des hommes,* the contrast between the airman, discovering through flight unsuspected aspects of the earth, and the travellers below who only get a very partial view of it, is made the subject of a simile which relates the very twentieth-century experience of flight to a kind of story-book past: 'Nous ressemblions à cette souveraine qui désira visiter ses sujets et connaître s'ils se réjouissaient de son règne. Ses courtisans, afin de l'abuser, dressèrent sur son chemin quelques heureux décors et payèrent des figurants pour y danser. Hors du mince fil conducteur, elle n'entrevit rien de son royaume, et ne sut point qu'au large des campagnes ceux qui mouraient de faim la maudissaient' (*TH,* p. 54). This simile is colourful but incoherent. The earthbound traveller is not the victim of a deliberate deception but of a truncated perspective and consequently, the deceitful courtiers and the hired entertainers acquire a sort of autonomous life of their own inside a fairy-tale that may be expressive of Saint-Exupéry's nostalgia for the past but which does little to illuminate the airman's original insight. This importing of a picturesque version of history into simile recurs in one of

Saint-Exupéry's descriptions of bad flying conditions, and proves equally strained and unconvincing: 'toutes les montagnes semblent au pilote rouler dans la crasse comme ces canons aux amarres rompues qui labouraient le pont des voiliers d'autrefois' (*TH,* p. 12). The crucial point about the first term of this comparison is that the mountains are in motion in the eyes of an airman struggling to ride out the storm. In the second term of the comparison, the human agent disappears and the mountains, figuratively 'adrift' in the sea of clouds, are, again colourfully, likened to the guns of ancient men-of-war which have broken away from their retaining ropes and slithered across the deck. Here again, the appeal to the 'romance' of the past has proved too strong for the simile and actually undermined its effectiveness as an image of the dangers of twentieth-century flying.

In singling out the way in which Saint-Exupéry's appeal to the past sometimes weakens the force and cohesion of his longer similes, I want to point to a related feature of his style which is also typical of his traditionalism. Concealed within the simile about the wild ducks, there is a parallel with the craving of human beings, as Saint-Exupéry interprets them, to ascend to some higher order of being. In essence, this is a *parable,* as is the story of the desert fox which forms part of Saint-Exupéry's ordeal in the Libyan desert. In this, you will recall, the fox's patience, caution and respect for the laws of natural life enable him to survive in a hostile environment by not exhausting his food supply. Saint-Exupéry concludes by drawing a lesson from the example of the desert fox: 'Et je reste là à rêver et il me semble que l'on s'adapte à tout. L'idée qu'il mourra peut-être trente ans plus tard ne gâte pas les joies d'un homme' (*TH,* p. 134).

This vein of parable is a stylistic feature of *Terre des hommes* which confirms that we are dealing with a novelist who is not only a moralist but also anxious to persuade us of the rightness of his views. In order to do so, he characteristically falls back on an almost archaic form of discourse that is rooted in the style of the New Testament. Not that Saint-Exupéry is an orthodox Catholic. Indeed, he seems to have abandoned the religious observances of his childhood quite early in his adult life and to have opened himself up to other philosophies, notably that of Nietzsche. Even so, it is difficult not to see, in the strenuous self-searching charted in the entries of his *Carnets,* that a naturally religious temperament is at work. At the very least, it can be said that Saint-Exupéry remained deeply affected by the example of the Christian religion and by the language of the Bible. Already, as a schoolboy, he could write to his mother in 1918: 'Je viens de lire un peu de Bible: quelle merveille, quelle simplicité puissante de style et quelle poésie souvent' (*Lettres,* p. 33).

Certainly, images drawn from religious life are scattered throughout the text of *Vol de nuit* and *Terre des hommes.* I have already referred to the imagery which tends to 'sanctify' the airman's vocation with its allusions to priesthood, baptism, consecration and renunciation. Elsewhere, especially in *Terre des hommes,* the language has resonances of a theological or Biblical kind, ranging from allusions to personal 'deliverance' – 'Comment favoriser en nous cette sorte de délivrance?' (*TH,* p. 158) – to others about the spiritual quickening of our dull mortal clay – 'Seul l'Esprit, s'il souffle sur la glaise, peut créer l'Homme' (p. 182) – or about the wrath of God: 'Il est des tempêtes de Dieu qui ravagent, ainsi, en une heure, les moissons d'un homme' (p. 100).

The concentrated 'stories' implicit in the parables, like Saint-Exupéry's succinct sentences with their Biblical flavour, already point toward a more general stylistic tendency which characterises *Vol de nuit* and *Terre des hommes.* This is the fondness for *aphorism,* which one can define as a condensed and memorable moral observation. It could be said that the pointed character of aphorism is already present in some of the sentences which make up the parables – 'S'il n'y avait point d'escargots, il n'y aurait point de fénechs', for example – but its use is in no sense restricted to these limited contexts. On the contrary, aphorism emerges as an important stylistic feature of both works. It contributes to the compactness and economy of *Vol de nuit,* is almost the governing stylistic principle of Rivière's many utterances, and is prominent in the long, reflective passages of *Terre des hommes.* Examples abound. Much of the moral significance which

Saint-Exupéry seeks to elicit from Guillaumet's ordeal in the Andes is encapsulated in the form of aphorisms: 'Seul l'inconnu épouvante les hommes' (*TH*, p. 47), for example; or 'Etre homme, c'est précisément être responsable' (ibid.). Elsewhere in *Terre des hommes,* we read: 'La grandeur d'un métier est peut-être, avant tout, d'unir des hommes' (p. 35), and: 'L'homme se découvre quand il se mesure avec l'obstacle' (p. 9).

The aphorisms scattered throughout the text of *Vol de nuit* are, as one might expect, most frequently placed in the mouth of Rivière, where they achieve a marked consistency. One recalls notably: 'Le règlement... est semblable aux rites d'une religion qui semblent absurdes mais façonnent les hommes' (*VN,* p. 46), and: 'Aimez ceux que vous commandez. Mais sans le leur dire' (p. 64), and again: 'Aimer, aimer seulement, quelle impasse!' (p. 131). In all these examples, Saint-Exupéry's recourse to aphorism may indeed denote a preference for pithiness and economy, but I suspect its significance is greater than this implies. It lies in his unavowed passion to convince the reader, to formulate and communicate a moral code that he will be prompted to ponder on and accept as valid. Here too Saint-Exupéry recalls Nietzsche who declared in *Thus Spoke Zarathustra*: 'He who writes in blood and aphorisms does not want to be read, he wants to learned by heart' (*4,* p. 67).

But though Saint-Exupéry's use of simile and aphorism helps to define an important aspect of the style of *Vol de nuit* and *Terre des hommes,* it cannot of itself account adequately for the dominant impression made on us by the prose of these two texts. What principally strikes us is a kind of vibrant poetic tone which stems in part from a sense of moral urgency in the work, but also from the frequency and colour of Saint-Exupéry's images. These often embody a powerful fusion of concrete and abstract, of material and spiritual. In the concluding part of this chapter, I want to look at these clusters of images and to explore how they work in the text. It will be convenient to begin with the most numerous and pervasive: the images of light and dark.

The dichotomy between light and dark is central to the narrative of *Vol de nuit* and a significant feature of *Terre des hommes*. The accumulated images of light, which spring initially from the special conditions of night flying, lend what one can only call a distinctive sheen to the surface of Saint-Exupéry's prose in *Vol de nuit* and, in a lesser degree, to some of the episodes retailed in *Terre des hommes*. This sheen overlying portions of the text is an essentially visual effect, but the images which account for it also carry a richer burden of meaning because they tap subterranean sources of personal sensibility and moral thought.

In Saint-Exupéry's writing, light is predominantly associated with positive values. It is linked to notions of the value of communication and of the preciousness of human community. It is also related to ideas of sustenance and nurture, security and protection. Commonly, the lights of human settlement (towns or villages or scattered farmhouses) are seen as symbolising the longed-for community in which the creative energies and mutual dependence of human beings are expressed. Sometimes the fragility of such communities is obliquely suggested. For example, the township of San Julian is portrayed as a mere speck of light and life in the surrounding dark: 'n'était plus qu'une poignée de lumières' (*VN*, p. 20). At other times, these lights, which are the proof of human habitation, are also associated with men and women reaching out to each other in a spirit of mutual aid: 'La terre était tendue d'appels lumineux, chaque maison allumant son étoile, face à l'immense nuit, ainsi qu'on tourne un phare vers la mer' (*VN*, p. 21). Nowhere is the idea of the preciousness of human community more sumptuously expressed than in the pages devoted to the passengers flying down from Paraguay and approaching the city of Buenos Aires. I have already touched on this passage as giving voice to the pilot's instrumental view of the world, but the images convey more than that. The little towns slip by below and the passengers see them as through the 'jeweller's window' of the plane (*VN*, p. 181). The lights of these townships are strung out like a 'gold necklace' under the paler gold of the stars, and the approaching city itself is a glittering treasure-house of precious stones. Here the picture of a fabulous hoard has the alluring character of a fairy-tale, while the successive images of silver and gold breathe a spirit of joy and optimism (7, p. 53).

These particular images, strongly expressive of the value of community, are prolonged and reinforced by a series of images of light which are associated with all that sustains and nurtures life. It is not simply that the lights of towns are sometimes referred to as 'living stars' (*TH*, p. 10), or that the helpful moonlight is represented as an inexhaustible 'fontaine de lumière' (*VN*, p. 118) from which, figuratively, the airman draws life. It is also that light is identified as the spirit of creativity, that which brings life out of uncreating darkness: 'L'or est né du Néant: il rayonne dans les feux de l'escale' (*TH*, p. 22).

In the same affirmative spirit, images of light are linked to notions of security and protection, and some of these gain an added resonance from the fact that they call on Saint-Exupéry's own experiences of childhood, experiences that continue to vivify his imagination as a writer. The settled life of home is epitomised in the beautiful image of 'le sanctuaire d'or des lampes du soir' (*VN*, p. 130), an image that has its roots in the childhood rituals of bedtime recalled by Saint-Exupéry in the letter written to his mother from Buenos Aires in 1930, and which I have already quoted. These rituals, framed in the peace and security childhood, are revived more directly in Saint-Exupéry's description of dinner at the old, crumbling mansion near Concordia: 'Et surtout j'aimais le transport des lampes. De vraies lampes lourdes, que l'on charriait d'une pièce à l'autre, comme aux temps les plus profonds de mon enfance, et qui remuaient aux murs des ombres merveilleuses. On soulevait en elles des bouquets de lumière et de palmes noires. Puis, une fois les lampes bien en place, s'immobilisaient les plages de clarté, et ces vastes réserves de nuit tout autour, où craquaient les bois' (*TH*, pp. 70-71). Here, not only does the reference to 'de vraies lampes lourdes' suggest how Saint-Exupéry identifies reality and solidity with childhood, but the light from the original memories of childhood elides imperceptibly into an essentially

marine image of a beach, with its implication of a storm-
tossed sailor reaching the safety of the shore, an image clearly
linked to the writer's adult flying experiences. It is these
memories of childhood, and of the child's need for security
and protection, that bring a certain plangency to some of the
images of light which the writer deploys. For example, they
infiltrate, and give life to, the scene in which Saint-Exupéry,
as a green novice, sits down to listen to the veteran Guillaumet's practical advice: 'Et, penché sous la lampe, appuyé à
l'épaule de l'ancien, je retrouvai la paix du collège' (*TH,*
p. 15). In the term 'l'ancien', the older flier is fused with the
senior boy of Saint-Exupéry's boarding school and a whole
area of childhood feeling and dependence and hero-worship
is imported into the adult scene.

However, images of light are plurivalent in Saint-
Exupéry's text. Though most of them are associated with
nurture, succour and human community, there is also a range
of images that evoke light as sterility, deception and danger.
Something of the specific character of such images derives
from the airman's encounter with the hazards of flight. In this
perspective, light is viewed instrumentally, in terms of the
operational needs of the flier. When the narrator of *Vol de
nuit* writes: 'Les plaines devenaient lumineuses mais d'une
inusable lumière' (p. 17), we can judge that we have moved
from a purely contemplative or aesthetic view of nature to a
more practical stance. However 'luminous' the plains, the
light they give off has no practical advantage for the flier
himself at the moment he is reporting on it. The same
instrumental view of flying works against the initial reverence
for the vastness and mystery of nature which Rivière feels at
one point in the action. Engine trouble in one of the aircraft
will necessitate delays to his schedule and he expresses his
frustration at this setback: '"Une telle nuit qui se perd!" Il
regardait avec rancune, par la fenêtre, ce ciel découvert,
enrichi d'étoiles, ce balisage divin, cette lune, l'or d'une telle
nuit dilapidé' (*VN,* p. 64). Once again, the sense of the sky as
beautiful recedes before the imperatives of operational flying.
There is a further example of this way of handling the
imagery of light. Weather reports from the north indicate

perfect flying conditions: 'mais leurs "ciels purs", leurs "pleine lune", et leurs "vent nul" éveillaient l'image d'un royaume stérile. Un désert de lune et de pierres' (*VN*, p. 175). These favourable indices are 'sterile' because they are of no help to the beleagured Fabien flying up from the storm-racked south. But the most amply developed use of this image of light as an emblem of sterility occurs at the most crucial moment in Fabien's desperate struggle with the storm. He climbs higher and higher and reaches a kind of luminous limbo, only to recognise it is all just an illusion of calm ('Trop beau'). Surrounded by this brilliant light, Fabien realises he and his navigator are doomed: 'Pareils à ces voleurs des villes fabuleuses, murés dans la chambre aux trésors dont ils ne sauront plus sortir. Parmi des pierreries glacées, ils errent, infiniment riches, mais condamnés' (*VN*, p. 145). Here the cold, concentrated light of this fabulous treasure, with its overtones of an Aladdin's cave, is the negative counterpart of the treasure-house of Buenos Aires that, later in the narrative, will be the cause of elation.

These images of sterility are closely allied with others which associate light, not with hope and safety but with danger and deception. Such images can be direct and almost homely, like that of Fabien's exhaust flame in the early stages of the storm: 'Elle était tressée drue par le vent, comme la flamme d'une torche' (*VN*, p. 110). At this point, the normally comforting connotations of 'torche' as a light to guide one are undermined by the unnerving oddity of that vertical flame that speaks so graphically of the force of the wind. Here, light is danger; elsewhere, it is a deception. As he waits for the overdue Fabien, Rivière 'jugeait les étoiles trop luisantes, l'air trop humide. Quelle nuit étrange! Elle se gâtait brusquement par plaques, comme la chair d'un fruit lumineux' (*VN*, p. 122). In this instance, the sudden transition from the inorganic (light) to the organic (decaying fruit) presents us with an audaciously wide-angled figure in which an unexpected verbal juxtaposition threatens the reader's confidence and opens up a new and menacing possibility. And these images of deceptive light accumulate in the pages leading up to Fabien's final crisis, increasing our sense of

unease. In the midst of the storm, he catches a glimpse of a
few stars in a clear patch of sky and likens them to a deadly
bait: 'un appât mortel au fond d'une nasse' (*VN,* p. 139). He
suspects the worst but the lure of the (normally beneficent)
light proves too strong: 'Mais sa faim de lumière était telle
qu'il monta' (p. 139). He climbs further, reaches 'des champs
de lumière' where the blinding light has transformed the
clouds into 'vagues rayonnantes' (*VN,* p. 144). Below him,
the storm still rages but, at the altitude at which he finds
himself, it produces a deceptive effect of marmoreal calm:
'elle tournait vers les astres une face de cristal et de neige'
(p. 144). It is all a mirage, and when the plane is depicted as
bathed in 'un lait de lumière' (p. 144), the nourishing and
comforting associations of milk are at variance with the cold
reality all around.

The intensity of images of light is in direct proportion to
the threat and fear generated by darkness. Darkness and night
really seem to come alive in *Vol de nuit.* The vivid and
concrete impressions we are given of the cyclone tend, as a
general effect, to merge the wind-currents and clouds with the
surrounding blackness. These terrifying motions of the air,
sometimes likened to tumultuous seas, sometimes to sudden
landslides, are doubly frightening because they take place in
the dark. Hence, fear of the dark and ordeal by darkness seem
to prevail. We can observe here how childhood fears of the
dark, magnified by Saint-Exupéry's reading about life under-
ground in Jules Verne's *Les Indes noires,* are transposed into
the pilot's struggle with the night. Night is the dimension of
test and trial, and must be mastered if hopes of a life-
enhancing network of communications are to be realised.
From this, one can understand that the challenge of night
flying, when first met by the novice pilot, may be seen as one
of attraction and repulsion. Saint-Exupéry writes of biting
into 'la pulpe amère des nuits de vol' (*TH,* p. 17). In this,
another example of a wide-angled, organic figure, the face of
the night is compared to the skin of a fruit. It has to be
broached, and there is anticipated pleasure, but the experience may well turn 'sour' on the pilot. For Rivière, however,
for whom such a network of communications is the proper

goal of a common effort, a sky at night that is not traversed by his pilots is simply emptied of significance, a reaction which he expresses in one of *Vol de nuit*'s rare theatrical similes: 'Rivière sortit pour tromper l'attente, et la nuit lui apparut vide comme un théâtre sans acteur' (*VN*, p. 64).

In *Vol de nuit* night is sometimes, rather conventionally, represented as a pit, either directly – 'Je me sentais au fond d'un grand trou dont il était difficile de remonter' (pp. 101-102) – or more obliquely: 'il frissonna de se sentir descendre au coeur de la nuit, sans secours, sous la seule protection d'une petite lampe de mineur' (p. 70). In a more general sense, darkness (the total absence of light) is equated with death. Such is the implication of the language used by Fabien's radio-operator as he looks down on the blackness below: 'l'espace dévasté, aux villes ensevelies, aux lumières mortes' (*VN*, p. 136). Yet, if the general impression created by *Vol de nuit* is of the frightening power of darkness, faithfully reflecting in this the hazards of the pioneering airmen, there are scattered moments in that novel, and in *Terre des hommes*, where a sense of reverence in the face of the majesty of creation overrides the fears of man. It is entirely characteristic of the vein of spirituality present in both texts that Saint-Exupéry should convey this sense of awe in the trite image of the cathedral – 'comme une vaste nef' (*VN*, p. 58). The rather tired and secondhand image may reflect the uncertain and unfocused nature of the spiritual concerns expressed in these writings.

We can now turn to Saint-Exupéry's sea images. These rival in importance his imagery of light, and one American critic even thinks of them as embodying a 'stylistic dominant' in his work (*12*, p. 34). Scrutiny of these sea images confirms that, though they are prolific in a prose marked by a wealth of similes, analogies and metaphors, they also tend, like the writer's images of light, to lack inventiveness and originality. Generally, they confine themselves to variants, sometimes ingenious and occasionally moving, on two basic figures: the sky as sea and the plane as ship. Both of these are traditional and commonplace, and are not less so when transposed to the desert, given the hackneyed nature of expressions like a 'sea

of sand'. In order to rescue his sea imagery from triteness,
Saint-Exupéry opens up the figure so as to accommodate a
burden of feeling that is linked with the terrors of night
flying.

It would be tedious to enumerate all the occasions when
Saint-Exupéry exploits the basic figure of the sky as sea, but a
few examples will serve to characterise his practice as a
writer. Operating well within a familiar convention, the
narrator refers to the winds: 'car les vents poussaient du Sud
vers le Nord leur grande houle favorable' (*VN*, p. 58).
Elsewhere the usage can be even more trite: 'cet océan de
ténèbres' (*TH*, p. 9), or 'des mers de nuages' (*TH*, p. 13), and
this hackneyed usage is hardly affected by the rather perfunc-
tory mythifying of the sea which Saint-Exupéry resorts to in
one instance: 'une ombrageuse divinité' (*TH*, p. 157). Nor
does the basic figure emerge with any compelling force or
freshness when it is applied to the land: 'Quelquefois, après
cent kilomètres de steppes plus inhabitées que la mer, il
croisait une ferme perdue, et qui semblait emporter en
arrière, dans une houle de prairies, sa charge de vies humaines, alors il saluait des ailes ce navire' (*VN*, p. 18).

More interesting is the attempt to expand the figure of
sea/ship in order to convey a larger sense of human destiny.
One example of this is the occasion in *Terre des hommes*
where, in a telling ellipsis, mineral and marine images are
juxtaposed in such a way as to shock us into a new awareness
of the earth as man's floating home in space. The narrator
lies in the desert, looking up at the heavens, and the pull of
gravity under his shoulders is surprisingly likened to 'ce pont
courbe de mon navire' (*TH*, p. 63), the demonstrative adjec-
tive signalling here, as so often in Saint-Exupéry, the metaphoric sense of what follows. He returns to this figure a little
later when the narrator, still stranded in the desert, compares
his situation to lying out on the upper deck during his voyage
out to South America: 'Il manque ici un mât, mais je suis
embarqué quand même, vers une destination qui ne dépend
plus de mes efforts. Des négriers m'ont jeté, lié, sur un navire'
(*TH*, p. 145). In this example, however, the novelettish
reference to the narrator as a slave on a slave ship is forced,

extraneous and does nothing to increase the suggestiveness of the image of 'sailing' across the sands. When Saint-Exupéry again resorts to this image of the earth as a ship on which mankind is riding, he shows himself too anxious to spell out his moral message: 'Nous sommes solidaires, emportés par la même planète, équipage d'un même navire' (*TH*, p. 175). That anxiety betrays an excess of timidity about the use of metaphor, and a tendency to adopt too didactic a stance in his attitude to us as readers.

Characteristically, it is only when Saint-Exupéry uses sea imagery in connection with the hazards of night flying that he manages to make such images appear to be the natural vehicle for conveying a vital experience. It is darkness, the realm of struggle, hope and fear, that endows his sea imagery with true potency. In identifying darkness with images of the sea, Saint-Exupéry sometimes conjures up the figure of the swimmer or diver plumbing the depths ('sonder l'espace'). For example, Fabien, after checking his instruments, prepares for 'son entrée dans la nuit, comme une plongée' (*VN*, p. 22), while elsewhere, pilots on their descent are likened to 'des plongeurs de métier' (*TH*, p. 21). This image works success-fully because it suggests economically both the boundlessness of space, the sense of the unknown, and the loneliness of the human agent. Curiously, it is all the more powerful when transferred from its normal setting (the night sky) to the silent night-time offices of the airline. The duty clerk, who answers the telephone that links his with the pilot's world of darkness and danger, returns to the circle of light cast on his desk by a lamp: 'comme un nageur entre deux eaux, revenant de l'ombre vers sa lampe' (*VN*, p. 79). This figure surprises us because of the elliptical way in which the beckoning light on the desk is made to connect with the 'sea' darkness around it and, by implication, with the larger sea of darkness outside in which Fabien is adrift.

The picture of night as the province of danger is normally expressed in conventional terms, as in the marine image exploited by Fabien when he notes: 'La nuit, et tout ce qu'elle portait de rocs, d'épaves, de collines, coulait aussi contre l'avion avec la même étonnante fatalité' (*VN*, p. 111). But the

most poetic, though still conventional, use of sea imagery is
that which connects the perilous 'sea' of darkness with the
prospect of a safe haven. Such images are perfectly congruent
with the sense of relief experienced by the flier as he is freed
from fear and immediate danger. I think particularly of
Pellerin's plane flying in from Chile and nearing the end of
its journey: 'la nuit en livrait un déjà, ainsi qu'une mer,
pleine de flux et de reflux et de mystères, livre à la plage le
trésor qu'elle a si longtemps ballotté' (*VN,* p. 28). Here the
plane is that 'treasure' soon to be safely washed up on the
welcoming 'beach' of the airfield at Buenos Aires. The same
figure recurs, instinct with the same feeling of release: 'Pour
le pilote, cette nuit était sans rivage... Fabien pensait à l'aube
comme à une plage de sable doré où l'on se serait échoué
après cette nuit dure' (*VN,* p. 113). In this case, the safe
haven offered by the beach is fused with the clement, golden
light of dawn. Such images can be moving but they remain
essentially conventional and familiar. Only once, it seems to
me, does Saint-Exupéry expand his sea imagery in such a way
as to arrest our attention and make us see the world afresh. I
refer to the moment when we are shown the pilot scheduled
for the European run lying asleep on his bed: 'Il reposait dans
ce lit calme, comme dans un port, et, pour que rien n'agitât
son sommeil, elle effaçait du doigt ce pli, cette ombre, cette
houle, elle apaisait ce lit, comme, d'un doigt divin la mer'
(*VN,* p. 93). This episode is clearly saturated with Saint-
Exupéry's childhood memories of the bedtime rituals presided over by his mother, but what is striking is the way in
which the image of night flying as a sea of darkness traversed
by the pilot/mariner is carried over into a domestic setting, so
that the airman's secure bed is made to evoke the safe haven
of a storm-tossed sailor, with the wife playing the part of a
mythological goddess who covers the flier with her protection.

In Saint-Exupéry's work, images of light and water are
associated with movement and life, even if the life of the
elements sometimes threatens human survival. The transpar-
ency and living flow of these images are contrasted in the text
with the opacity and sterility of the mineral world. At its

limit, the imagery of this world is the imagery of death. Nothing illustrates this more dramatically than the scene in *Terre des hommes* (p. 135) where the half-delirious narrator encounters a petrified forest in the desert. In a series of metamorphoses, depicted with brilliant economy, life is converted into death before his very eyes: 'mais cet homme qui gesticulait n'était qu'un rocher noir'; and 'ce Bédouin qui dormait... s'est changé en tronc d'arbre noir'; and again: 'Je veux soulever une branche brisée: elle est de marbre!' The petrified forest is strewn about him like a 'cathedral' that has collapsed in ruins. All life has departed from it: 'Cette forêt, qui fut pleine d'oiseaux et de musique a été frappée de malédiction et changée en sel'. The spectacle prompts him to ask rhetorically: 'Qu'ai-je à faire ici, moi, vivant, parmi ces marbres incorruptibles? Moi, périssable, moi, dont le corps se dissoudra, qu'ai-je à faire ici dans l'éternité?'

This impresses me as a passage of great beauty and effectiveness, but not because of any novelty in the language – indeed, it reads a little like a pastiche of classical French prose. But it is memorable for its imaginative intensity. It combines echoes of the evil spells that happen in fairy-tales with echoes of the Bible (Lot's wife turned into a pillar of salt). It not only sounds a moving elegy over flora and fauna that have vanished for ever, but expresses, in its final juxta-position of mortality and eternity, a kind of dignity and solemnity reminiscent of the great pulpit oratory of the past. There are, of course, more general images of desolate places in *Vol de nuit* and *Terre des hommes,* but none that captures so hauntingly the gap between human transience and vulner-ability, on the one hand, and the implacable permanence of natural phenomena, on the other. Something of this stark opposition is, however, present in another of Saint-Exupéry's encounters in the desert. This is when he comes across a mass of shiny black pebbles which he identifies, with a thrill of intellectual pride and excitement, as long-fallen meteors. The poetic conceit he employs for describing this mineral litter – 'coulé en forme de larme' (*TH,* p. 61) – is in itself further proof of the power of the human imagination to bring together things which might otherwise be thought of as

distinct and remote from each other. In combining the shape
of tear drops with the solid blackness of the mineral, the
writer creates a funereal image, perhaps echoing the jet cos-
tume-jewellery conventionally worn during periods of
mourning by women in his childhood, which graphically
suggests a sense of mourning for the meteors' fall from
incandescent light into the mineral 'dark'. But this striking
conceit is weakened when Saint-Exupéry grafts organic imagery on to his extended description of the meteor-strewn
landscape. He thus transforms the black pebbles into the fruit
of a heavenly tree: 'je pensais que, du haut de ce pommier
céleste devaient avoir chu d'autres fruits' (p. 61). This seems
to me a case of not knowing when to leave well alone, for the
pebbles, as the 'fruit' of a 'tree' in the sky, jar with the
death-haunted figure he has already created.

In the patterns of imagery deployed by Saint-Exupéry in
*Vol de nuit* and *Terre des hommes,* it is sea images and
images of light and dark which predominate. Mineral images,
though memorably handled, play a much lesser part, even if
the metaphor of the desert as the privileged realm of human
struggle and self-realisation might properly be said to haunt
*Terre des hommes.* Only one other image seems to me to be
significant, that of music. It occurs rarely, mostly in *Vol de
nuit,* but is often crucially placed and can be powerfully
suggestive of some of Saint-Exupéry's concerns. A handful of
examples comes to mind. In the first, Rivière recalls stormy
nights ('nuits de désordre') when planes are in difficulties. On
such occasions, the plane's radio emits its 'plainte mêlée au
grésillement des orages. Sous cette gangue sourde, l'or de
l'onde musicale se perdait. Quelle détresse dans le chant
mineur d'un courrier jeté en flèche aveugle vers les obstacles
de la nuit!' (*VN,* p. 59). In this instance, music (the order of
art) is set against the storm (the disorder of the elements), and
the musical figure itself translates, through the minor key, the
doubts and anxieties of the crew. The second example occurs
when Fabien is given up for lost. The ground radio still
struggles to maintain contact but now its signals sound like a
lament: 'Seule relie encore Fabien au monde une onde
musicale, une modulation mineure. Pas une plainte. Pas un

cri. Mais le son le plus pur qu'ait jamais formé le désespoir' (p. 155). Here the minor key, conventionally associated with moods of sadness, points, with admirable discretion, to Fabien's end. The order of art is found to be powerless against the catastrophes of nature. It can only register defeat, though a defeat mitigated by the solicitude and solidarity of all those involved in the common struggle.

Conversely, when the plane from Asunción lands safely, the radio-operator's last messages are lent the shaping finality of art: 'Le radio, de ses doigts, lâchait les derniers télégrammes, comme les notes finales d'une sonate qu'il eût tapotée, joyeux, dans le ciel, et dont Rivière comprenait le chant' (*VN*, p. 182). And when the mail-plane for Europe eventually takes off, its passage overhead is compared to the triumphant peal of an organ – 'un chant d'orgue' (p. 188). To close the narrative with a musical figure suggests the importance which the author gives to such a figure in shaping the text. And that significance comes from equating the radio (one form of communication) with music (a greater form of human communication) and from seeing in both a desire to draw mankind together and to remind them of their common humanity.

# Conclusion

CHAPTER 5 subsumes much of Saint-Exupéry's practice as a writer, as we have been able to trace it in previous chapters. It confirms that in *Vol de nuit* and *Terre des hommes* Saint-Exupéry moves by analogy, simile and image, by a multiplicity of vivid fragments. In a word, he moves by poetic, rather than novelistic, processes, which is why the American critic quoted earlier thinks of him primarily as 'a poet and a sea-haunted one' (*12*, p. 43). I would agree that something of the poet's approach and much of the poet's intensity of feeling are at work in these texts, though I think that the imagery of light and dark must be seen as rivalling in importance his sea images. But if the poetic dimension is one of the most distinctive features of the texts, it cannot adequately define them. There are other vital elements which help to give them their special identity.

The first of these is the author's marvellously exact eye for the concrete detail of flying, especially in *Vol de nuit*. Second, there is his gift for awakening us to a new awareness of the planet that is our home. Finally, there is his capacity for exciting our moral imagination, even when we are not able fully to assent to his prescriptions for our moral regeneration or to accept the traditionalist picture of society and of the relations between men and women that he presents us with. Yet, whatever their intrinsic value, these elements cannot be said to reflect the skills and interests of the true novelist. Saint-Exupéry evinces little ability to build and sustain a large fictional structure; to articulate and elaborate a plot; to invent a range of characters and show them interacting with each other; or to develop and amplify, rather than simply reiterate, his chosen themes.

It has to be said that the injunction to 'make it new', which inspires so much significant art and literature of the twentieth century, has passed Saint-Exupéry by. In matters of literary technique, he is no innovator, but he has contrived a hybrid literary form in which elements of adventure story, spiritual autobiography and moral fable are combined, always interestingly, and often arrestingly. In this form of prose writing, a few deeply held insights into moral and social life are urged on us with a rhetorical eloquence which can be moving but which is also, it must be confessed, rather dated. In spite of these reservations, *Vol de nuit* and *Terre des hommes* continue to exert a spell over their readers, a spell that is intimately linked with the passage of time. From the vantage point of the 1990s, the airmen who dominate these pages emerge as luminous and exemplary figures who somehow transcend the wars, economic crises and political terror of the interwar years. With the lapse of time, they have become truly legendary and, through them, we can recognise the claims of courage, generosity and idealism and share in the author's passionate concern to reclaim mankind from the dehumanising pressures of the twentieth century.

# Select Bibliography

A. EDITIONS OF SAINT-EXUPÉRY'S WORK

*Œuvres* (Paris, Bibliothèque de la Pléiade, 1959).
*Œuvres complètes,* 7 vols (Paris, Editions du Club de l'Honnête Homme, 1985-86).
*Cahiers Saint-Exupéry,* I (Paris, Gallimard, 1980). Reprints some inaccessible material.
*Carnets,* ed. P. Chevrier ('Collection Soleil', Paris, Gallimard, 1975).
*Ecrits de guerre, 1939-1944,* ed. L. Evrard (Paris, Gallimard, 1982).
*Lettres de Saint-Exupéry,* édition revue et corrigée (Paris, Le Club du Meilleur Livre, 1960).
*Un Sens à la vie,* ed. Cl. Reynal (Paris, Gallimard, 1956).


B. BIOGRAPHICAL AND BACKGROUND STUDIES

* *1.* Curtis Cate, *Antoine de Saint-Exupéry: his life and times* (London, Heinemann, 1970).
* *2.* René Delange, *La Vie de Saint-Exupéry* (Paris, Seuil, 1948).
  *3.* Marcel Migeo, *Saint-Exupéry* (London, Macdonald, 1961).
  *4.* Friedrich Nietzsche, *Thus Spoke Zarathustra,* trans. R.J. Hollingdale (Harmondsworth, Penguin Books, 1961).
  *5.* Richard Rumbold & Margaret Stewart, *The Winged Life: a portrait of Antoine de Saint-Exupéry, poet and airman* (London, Weidenfeld & Nicolson, 1953).


C. CRITICAL STUDIES

* *6.* R.-M. Albérès *et al., Saint-Exupéry* (Paris, Hachette, 1963).
* *7.* Daniel Anet, *Antoine de Saint-Exupéry: poète, romancier, moraliste* (Paris, Corrêa, 1946).
  *8.* Germaine Brée & Margaret Guiton, *The French Novel from Gide to Camus* (New York, Harbinger Books, 1962), pp. 193-203.
* *9.* Pierre Chevrier, *Saint-Exupéry* (Paris, Gallimard, 1958).
  *10.* Luc Estang, *Saint-Exupéry par lui-même* (Paris, Seuil, 1956).

*11.* C. François, *L'Esthétique de Saint-Exupéry* (Neuchâtel/Paris, Delachaux et Niestlé, 1957).

*\* 12.* W. M. Frohock, *Style and Temper: studies in French fiction 1925-1960* (Oxford, Blackwell, 1967), pp. 31-44.

*13.* J.-C. Ibert, *Antoine de Saint-Exupéry* (Paris, Editions Universitaires, 1960).

*\* 14.* R. Ouellet, *Les Relations humaines dans l'œuvre de Saint-Exupéry* (Paris, Minard, 1971).

*15.* Henri Peyre, *The Contemporary French Novel* (New York, O.U.P., 1955), pp. 151-81.

*16.* J. D. M. Robinson, *Antoine de Saint-Exupéry* ('Twayne World Authors', Boston, Hall, 1984).

*\* 17.* P.-H. Simon, *L'Homme en procès* (Neuchâtel, A la Baconnière, 1950), pp. 125-54.

*\* 18.* Colin Smith, *Contemporary French Philosophy: a study in norms and values* (London, Methuen, 1964), pp. 232-45.

*19.* C. L. Van den Berghe, *La Pensée de Saint-Exupéry* (New York/Berne/Frankfurt, Peter Lang, 1985).

*\* 20.* Michael T. Young, *Saint-Exupéry: 'Vol de nuit'* ('Studies in French Literature', London, Edward Arnold, 1971).

\* An asterisk indicates those titles which I have found most helpful for the purposes of this study.

# CRITICAL GUIDES TO FRENCH TEXTS

*edited by*
Roger Little, Wolfgang van Emden, David Williams

61. **Geoffrey N. Bromiley.** Thomas's Tristan *and the* Folie Tristan d'Oxford.
62. **R.J. Howells.** Rousseau: Julie ou la Nouvelle Héloïse.
63. **George Evans.** Lesage: Crispin rival de son maître *and* Turcaret.
64. **Paul Reed.** Sartre: La Nausée.
65. **Roger McLure.** Sarraute: Le Planétarium.
66. **Denis Boak.** Sartre: Les Mots.
67. **Pamela M. Moores.** Vallès: L'Enfant.
68. **Simon Davies.** Laclos: Les Liaisons dangereuses.
69. **Keith Beaumont.** Jarry: Ubu Roi.
70. **G.J. Mallinson.** Molière: L'Avare.
71. **Susan Taylor-Horrex.** Verlaine: Fêtes galantes *and* Romances sans paroles.
72. **Malcolm Cook.** Lesage: Gil Blas.
73. **Sheila Bell.** Sarraute: Portrait d'un inconnu *and* Vous les entendez?
74. **W.D. Howarth.** Corneille: Le Cid.
75. **Peter Jimack.** Diderot: Supplément au Voyage de Bougainville.
76. **Christopher Lloyd.** Maupassant: Bel-Ami.